A Survival Guide for Church Ministers

William J. Jarema

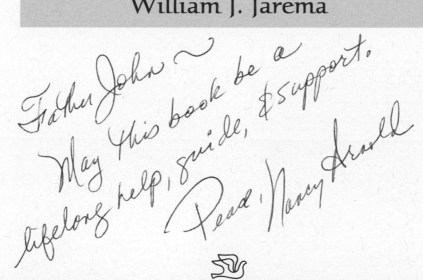

Fathu John ~
May this book be a
lifelong help, guide, & support.
Peace, Nancy Arnold

Paulist Press
New York/Mahwah, NJ

(Written by the founder of the center
in Colorado where I received much
wonderful help!)

Scripture texts in this work are taken from the *New American Bible with Revised New Testament and Revised Psalms* © 1991, 1986, 1970 Confraternity of Christian Doctrine, Washington, DC, and are used by permission of the copyright owner. All Rights Reserved. No part of the *New American Bible* may be reproduced in any form without permission in writing from the copyright owner.

The Publisher gratefully acknowledges use of the following materials:

The WART (Work Addiction Risk Test) and The Balance Wheel of Life in Chapter 15 are from Bryan E. Robinson, *Work Addiction: Hidden Legacies of Adult Children*. Copyright © 1989. Reprinted with permission of Heath Communications, Inc., www.hcibooks.com.

Deborah Tannen. *Talking 9 to 5: Facilitator's Guide*. Burnsville: ChartHouse International Learning Corporation, MN. Copyright © 1995 Deborah Tannen. Reprinted by permission.

"Overview of the Four Basic Types of Leadership Style" (pp. 126-7) from LIBERATING LEADERSHIP: PRACTICAL STYLES FOR PASTORAL MINISTRY by BERNARD SWAIN. Copyright © 1986 by Bernard F. Swain. Reprinted by permission of HarperCollins Publishers.

Material in online handout # 8 copyright © 1991, Bryan E. Robinson, *Heal Your Self Esteem: Recovery from Addictive Thinking* (Deerfield Beach, Florida: Health Communications). Used with permission.

Cover and book design by Lynn Else

Library of Congress Cataloging-in-Publication Data

Jarema, William J.
A survival guide for church ministers / William J. Jarema
    p. cm.
Includes bibliographical references (p.   ).
ISBN 978-0-8091-4721-2 (alk. paper)
1. Church management. 2. Church officers—Catholic Church. I. Title.
BV652.J37 2011
254—dc22

                                                                              2011001658

Published by Paulist Press
997 Macarthur Boulevard
Mahwah, New Jersey 07430

www.paulistpress.com

Printed and bound in the
United States of America

Contents

Contents

Online Resources: Access by selecting the Online Resources link
at www.paulistpress.com and then selecting the book title,
A Survival Guide for Church Ministers.

Introduction

In today's reality of church and diocese, we have become familiar with a new vocabulary that can be volatile and controversial. Ask any church member in the pew what is their understanding of:

Clustering parishes
Regional ministries
Single parishes with multiple worship sites
A pastor with four, five or six churches
Clergy and vocations shortage
Lay leadership training without diocesan finances and
    resources
Sunday service in the absence of a priest
New models of church leadership
Multicultural churches
Pastors with diocesan jobs in addition to their full parish
    schedules

As a Roman Catholic priest of twenty-eight years, I have come to see and experience the best and worst of church ministers and their attempts to safeguard and defend the precepts of the Roman Church and manage growth demands, aging buildings, expansive pastoral services, expansive ministries and paid personnel. Having worked with pastors from numerous other denominations, I can say that we as pastors, men and women, church staff, church volunteers and leadership councils all suffer from similar problems, pitfalls and professional liability when it comes to working *for* a particular church, *with* a particular church and *in* a particular church.

How do we equip those men and women who are in the trenches of church ministry doing their best with budget shortfalls, reduced

1

staff and volunteers, expanding church populations, and unrealistic expectations of a pastor's time, talents and energy? How do we practice a spirituality of longevity and avoid ministry burnout? Our definition of *leadership* and its applications will have a direct impact on what others can and will expect from us as pastors and church leaders.

Church leaders need to embrace the built-in evolution of change and be willing to update our own pastoral skills so that we can remain informed about the growing paradigm shifts around us and still feel effective in our field of expertise. How a man or woman pastors today has significant differences, expectations and measurable effectiveness compared to a short span of even twenty years ago.

My sister Theresa gave me *A Pictorial History of the Boyne Valley Area*, and I offer to you these 1915 rules of conduct for teachers of that day to make my point about pastoral evolution. The change process cannot be stopped. Rather, we adapt accordingly to the changes that occur willingly or suffer the consequences of being obsolete and out-of-touch and out-of-date.

In 1915 a teacher's magazine listed the following rules of conduct for teachers of that day:

1. You will not marry during the term of your contract.
2. You are not to keep company with men.
3. You must be home between the hours of 8:00 p.m. and 6:00 a.m. unless attending a school function.
4. You may not loiter downtown in ice cream stores.
5. You may not travel beyond the city limits unless you have the permission of the chairman of the board.
6. You may not ride in a carriage or automobile with any man unless he is your father or brother.
7. You may not smoke cigarettes.
8. You may not dress in bright colors.
9. You may under no circumstances dye your hair.
10. You must wear at least two petticoats.
11. Your dresses must not be any shorter than two inches above the ankle.
12. To keep the school room neat and clean, you must: sweep the floor once daily; scrub the floor at least once a week with hot, soapy water; clean the blackboards at least once

a day; and start the fire at 7:00 a.m. so the room will be warm by 8:00 a.m.[1]

Pastors, church leadership and ministry volunteers are under the common demand to evolve and learn effective leadership and management tools and techniques. Information is power for an effective parish leader. Today's pastor needs to be open to the numerous areas that can provide education and resources that assist him or her to be more effective in dealing with a multiplicity of issues: inclusion; multicultural awareness; sensitivity to special-needs populations; loss of employment or loved ones; mental, physical and spiritual health; single-parent units recovering from divorce, separation or death; the human longing to belong and to love and be loved; and, most of all, to worship and commune with the divine in a safe and loving environment.

Pastors are not permitted the luxury of ignorance of civil law. This means that today, pastors and church leaders are obligated to understand the complex legal, canonical, federal and state employee and health and safety regulations; HIPAA and OSHA directives; laws that protect employees from improper dismissal; sexual misconduct policies and mandatory reporting; and effective, adequate supervision of staff and volunteers (some who are better qualified than the pastor). How many classes in seminary did you get on business management, profit and loss statements, income and expense spreadsheets, employee management, building and environmental safety standards, school accreditation requirements, and personnel management and supervision? To fill the deficit for anyone who feels insecure in some of these areas, this book can help you.

This book has been written to support those men and women who want to embody our biblical way of life and encourage growth in a Christian faith and spirituality. Any man or woman who wants to be an effective Christian leader today needs a steady commitment to ongoing education that extends her/his collective studies in theology, philosophy and spirituality. Of all the skills that I believe the reader can glean from this book, I hope and pray that "common sense" be the cornerstone of what you gain from reading *A Survivor's Guide for Church Ministers*.

As a world community, we have evolved in our understanding of human rights, even though some countries fall far from the ideal. As a community of believers, we have struggled to empower women whom our founder, Jesus the Christ, called by name and maintained relationships with them that was countercultural and challenged the religious leaders of his times. As the body of Christ, how we care for and protect children, teenagers, the disabled and the elderly has created a purgative movement that has brought some churches, dioceses and countries to their knees in repentance and restitution.

Can we learn from the past so that we don't repeat it? A remembered past is a promise of a new future. Remembering the past speaks to the importance of taking hold of the pure and innocent charism of our founding fathers/mothers, looking to Jesus the Christ and measuring all that we do against what he himself has already done well.

Jesus associated freely with women and children. He ate with public sinners and those who lived on the edge of the religious community. Jesus never asked anybody to adore him or even acknowledge him as the Son of God. However, he did ask people to follow him and do what he did. He fed the hungry, healed the sick, touched the unloved, allowed himself to be touched and received the affections of those considered unworthy and unclean. Jesus defended his time alone while camping in the desert, boating and fishing with his disciples and recreating with family and friends. Those who could not understand such common-sense holiness called Jesus a "drunk and glutton." For those of us who practice and attempt to live "life…to the full" (John 10:10), we know for certain how important the art of self-care is to our lives, our churches and our congregations. There is nothing worse than an unhappy preacher encouraging the congregation to be happy when he/she has no joy of voice, posture or message.

As a preacher and conference speaker, I have jokingly said, "Please don't do what I do; rather, do as I say." I am not a billboard for physical or mental health. Yet I do believe that we need to become what we preach. Our embodiment of being balanced and healthy leaders speaks louder than the best sound system a church can install. How we care for our bodies, minds and spirits as good stewards of our personal investments makes for a great sermon. Jesus does this when he goes home to visit family and friends and proclaims his job description while attending temple.

When asked to share a reading from his ancestors in faith, Jesus picks up the scroll and reads from Isaiah 61:1–3:

The spirit of the LORD God is upon me,
because the LORD has anointed me;
He has sent me to bring glad tidings to the lowly,
to heal the brokenhearted,
To proclaim liberty to the captives
and release to the prisoners,
To announce a year of favor from the LORD
and a day of vindication by our God,
to comfort all who mourn;
To place on those who mourn in Zion
a diadem instead of ashes,
To give them oil of gladness in place of mourning,
a glorious mantle instead of a listless spirit.
They will be called oaks of justice,
planted by the LORD to show his glory.

Jesus completes his proclamation by saying that *today* this reading is fulfilled in your midst. Watch me put it into action.

Jesus preached so as to empower. His teachings were to lift people into the divine, not weigh them down with guilt and shame. His parables called forth the skills to wonder about the questions of life. In wondering, his audience came to realize that some life events are enveloped in mystery and do not have simple answers. Through his actions, Jesus invited those who wanted to dare and risk: "Don't just listen to what I say, but watch what I do. If you want to follow me then get in the boat and row; otherwise, get out and swim."

Every pastor and parish leader needs men, women and children who are willing to take up an oar and help row the boat. If the pastor or church leader can't hand over the oars, then the boat could end up going nowhere or crash into something one hoped could be avoided. A good leader helps with the rowing when needed, yet better serves the cause of the community by looking ahead and serving as the coxswain ("boat servant," meaning one who guides and motivates the rhythm of rowing and serves as the lookout). Making adjustments in the course of life and offering ways to make the workload lighter was a skill Jesus embodied. He never asked anyone to do what he did not do himself.

As we try to become whom we love—Jesus the Christ—and do our best to become good stewards of the treasures of others, may we be called "oaks of justice." Our family, friends and church members can rest their weary heads under the shade of our loving presence. Kids can climb the branches of our integrity and feel the strength we have to offer, and they can play in safety. Even the birds of the air can rest in our limbs and benefit from our well-being. Because we are rooted and grounded in a God of love, we can show others how to bend during the storm and adapt to the winds of time. We are intimately connected to the Creator who is the giver of all good gifts. We as disciples receive in abundance so that we can become generous distributors of what we have received. What you learn from this book share with everybody. Give away your insights and learned lessons, like bread broken and shared without condition or requirement.

Chapter 1
Men and Women in Ministry
Honoring the Differences

Men and women communicate differently. As gender is related to communication styles, so are issues of status and connection, hierarchy and equality, and closeness and distance. Deborah Tannen has researched how men and women use different communication styles in the workplace. Her books *You Just Don't Understand* and *Talking from 9 to 5* illustrate how men and women in a variety of employment situations will access different styles of communication that include variations in volume of voice ("It's not what you say but how you say it"), physical posture, intonation, eye contact, direct and indirect styles of giving orders, report versus rapport, sharing, greasing the wheels, small talk to create a flow of information, and ritual apologizing. Tannen illustrates how women try to link with coworkers and find what they have in common while men establish who are the high-status men and who are the low-status men.

Ways of talking do not in themselves have positive or negative value. Struggling to maintain the one-up position can work fine when everyone in the conversation is doing it, just as expending effort to maintain a conventionalized appearance of equality can work fine when everyone is doing it. However, problems arise when people's styles differ. Styles characteristic of many women put the speaker in a one-down position in conversations with those who have styles characteristic of men—especially in a work setting, where everyone is continually laboring under scrutiny, their performance and competence subject to judgment.[1]

How do church leaders create and sponsor an atmosphere that honors the talents and skills of each person who desires to embody our biblical way of life and encourage stewardship of the whole person? In today's church environment, how do church leaders honor the differences between men and women in the workplace? To begin to acknowledge the differences between men and women, Deborah Tannen establishes a basic premise.

> She states: Talk is one of the main ways people show the world their character and their worth. But the most important key is understanding the parameters of conversational style, which provides the tools to become more flexible not only in your own way of speaking but, equally important, in interpreting how others mean what they say, and in evaluating others' abilities. Understanding what goes on when people talk to each other is the best way to improve communication and get more work done—in the workplace as in all aspects of our lives.[2]

Conversational style is personal, shaped by cultural rules and fine-tuned by family beliefs and patterns of communication, whether functional or dysfunctional. Not all conversational styles are effective and may not produce the best results for a particular situation or desired outcome. Showing adaptability, understanding, empathy and patience in receiving another person's communication style is the core of any church leader, congregation staffer or volunteer dedicated to the divine ministry of hospitality.

Understanding the differences between men and women and how they communicate is not to feminize or emasculate the men or wrap women with a thin veneer of masculine overtones and aggressive behaviors. In most churches the majority of employees and volunteers are women. Pretending that women and men are the same hurts women, because the ways they are treated are often based on the norms for men. It also hurts men, who, with good intentions, speak to women as they would to men, and are nonplussed when their words don't work as they expected or even spark resentment and anger.[3]

Many male pastors and pastoral leaders have integrated communication skills that are inclusive and sensitive to women. Seminary formation and ongoing education has afforded both men and women's sensitivity to the multicultural reality of their churches. In doing so, a bright light has shown on the fact that women for centuries have been minimized in their contributions toward differentiating our religious and cultural understanding of power, leadership style, impact, pastoral care, inclusion, empathy and the feminine principle that defines beauty, power and nature independent of a man's definition or preference.

Deborah Tannen offers a chart in her video *Talking from 9 to 5.*[4] Every church throughout the world should consider obtaining this video and offer it to anyone who desires to work or serve with men and women within the church or congregation. The chart pictured below reveals that there are two continuums every person is working from in all communication exchanges. Both are useful. Neither is right or wrong. The question each person must ask: "Does your communication pattern help you achieve your desired goal?"

```
                    HIERARCHY
                        |
  CLOSENESS _____|_____ DISTANCE
                        |
                    EQUALITY
```

All four points on the communication continuum are useful when applied to the right situation, and being congruent with its application is the key to successful communications. Successful communication and effectiveness in conversational style can be achieved by learning the art and science of negotiating either more status or more connection.

Imagine you are at a meeting. If the goal of the meeting were to build relationships, the facilitator would want to emphasize closeness and equality. In these communication strategies, placing the chairs in a circle would suggest the equality of each group member's participation. Inviting people to share personal matters or concerns so as to create an environment of self-disclosure could achieve closeness.

If hierarchy and distance were desired, then the design of the room would be a traditional classroom setting. The teacher would be in the front and all the students would be facing the teacher and usually the chalkboard. Most churches are designed with a hierarchical design. The pews are all facing toward the presider's chair and altar. The celebrant is the leader and the congregation follows. If shared ministries are allowed, then you might see the choir director stand at the ambo/podium at certain times of worship. In measurement you would notice that the greater the distance between the teacher and student, the more formal the interactions between teacher and student.

Notice when it's time for a finance council meeting or school board meeting. It is typical that whoever leads sits up front and center stage. Information flows from the leader to the participants. The participants who ask questions would direct them to the person in charge. Personal sharing is reduced to the minimum while agenda items and the sharing of factual information become the primary matters discussed.

There are times when hierarchy and distance serve a purpose in helping to communicate and direct those involved. In matters of urgency, direct orders and knowing who is in charge could be a matter of life and death. In an emergency, a single person in charge can best facilitate and coordinate contributions from a group response. A leader relies on confidentiality (hierarchy and distance), limiting who has access to critical information. That is why it can be lonely at the top. The very position of being elected the leader does isolate and create a distance from regular work and ministry relationships.

Those men and women who were at one time just one of the gang and then become elected leaders can be jolted by their new job demands. Communication styles change to meet the new job dynamic. Coworkers expecting a friendly and informal communication style instead may be surprised by an approach that is more distant, formal and hierarchical. Leadership positions require an objectivity that is protected by distance, formality and autonomy from personal and group opinions and feelings.

If women speak and hear language of connection and intimacy while men speak and hear a language of status and independence, then communication between men and women can be like cross-cultural communication, prey to a clash of conversational styles. Instead of different dialects, it has been said they speak different genderlects.[5]

Conflict arises in a group or staff when some hear the language of closeness and equality while others hear the language of hierarchy and distance. When sameness is being reinforced, connection is being attempted. When position and influence are communicated, then status is being reinforced.

Protocol, guidelines, rules and reference to personnel manuals and instructions create an atmosphere of distance and hierarchy. Both status and connection can be used as communication strategies to get things done by talking. Both status and connection are ways of being involved with others and showing involvement with others, although those who are focused on one may not see the other as a means of involvement. Men are more often inclined to focus on the jockeying for status in conversation. Women are more often attuned to the negotiation of connections. Since both elements are always present, it is easy for women and men to focus on different elements in the same conversation.[6]

Men can use the connection strategy just as effectively as women, who, in turn, can capably employ the strategy of status. These communication strategies can be effective for both men and women. Each communication strategy can contribute to a desired outcome. How you apply each strategy and the degree of intensity that you use will influence the positive or negative benefits within the working relationship. Both connection and status are available for either gender.

Behavioral Markers

To begin with some simple behavioral markers for communication styles, think of how you embody and demonstrate the following:

1. *Volume*: On a scale of 1 to 10, how do you rate your volume of communication in a group conversation?

1	2	3	4	5	6	7	8	9	10
Barely Audible			Soft Spoken			Confident/Clear			Loud

2. *Pacing and pausing*: When you are trying to communicate something of importance, do you run roughshod through the conversation leaving little or no room for the other(s) to interject ideas or comments?

OR

Do you pause and let others confirm that what you are saying is understandable, and allow time for questions and clarification during your presentation?

3. *Direct versus indirect giving of orders*: Can you ask for what you want and give directions to accomplish your desired goals?

OR

Do you talk around what you have in mind and make suggestions with the hope that the person you are speaking with will get your drift?

4. *The use of questioning*: When you are seeking information from a coworker, do you ask closed-ended questions that limit their response to "yes" or "no"?

OR

Do you ask probing questions that encourage an exchange of information and promote dialogue and conversation?

5. *Ritual apologizing*: How many times during the day have you said, "I'm sorry"?

6. When you first meet with coworkers, do you take the time to "grease the wheels"? Do you make the effort to show interest in their lives, activities, health and interests before you move into business matters?

OR

Do you find that getting to work and passing on assignments and gleaning information to get the day's work started is your first line of action?

7. Would you say that most of your conversation is "report" talking or "rapport" sharing? Report talking would include an exchange of facts, activities, objective relating and impersonal information.

OR

Rapport sharing would include personal matters about your family, friends, life experiences and health, showing concern and interest through mutual self-disclosure.

8. Do you allow for playful teasing and joking in your workplace? Do the men in your workplace tend toward bantering and one-upmanship? Are you aware that the women in your workplace tend toward teasing and playful joking? What happens when jokes and teasing take on a sexually tinged humor? Have you noticed that when a group of men gather, they banter and use more aggression in their jokes? A gathering of women will joke about personal mistakes, tell stories about their failures and offer playful jokes and passive teasing. Women can also use sexually tinged humor.

9. When does the teasing and bantering from either males or females become inappropriate, if not even, sexually abusive or exploitive?

10. *Personal space, social space and boundaries*: Culture, family rules and professional training shapes our understanding of social space and boundaries. Are you aware of the eighteen to twenty-four inches around your body, and who and when do you allow others into this space? List the people, situations and how often you allow others into your personal space.

When you are in a professional role, are you aware of the differences of space and limits that protect how you keep people out of your social space? See chapter 2 on boundaries.

11. *Ritual opposition or being the devil's advocate*: Do you tend to argue for what is wrong or weak with a suggestion so as to reassure yourself that all the loose ends are tied up and, in the end, believe that the suggested idea can really take shape and be successful?

12. *Helpful criticism and useful feedback*: When providing feedback or criticism, do you spend adequate time emphasizing what has been good and useful, building on past strengths to help the person receiving the criticism seize this opportunity for personal growth and improvement?

13. *Speaking on behalf of you, "I" versus the group "we"*: When communication is exchanged between two people, a sacred place is created when "I" speaks to "I." This exchange of thoughts, feelings and ideas serves as the building blocks for future exchanges of information and begins to create familiarity. Familiarity opens the door to dependability that generates an awareness of safety. With safety the combination of giving and receiving through effective communication creates workplace intimacy. This is the platform required before trust can be established. When a person resorts to a power play and brings the invisible "we," defense mechanisms kick in, trust is annihilated, safety is violated and the lack of freedom to express what "I" think, feel and want is no longer a shared value between these two people.

Are you comfortable creating a sacred space and taking turns exchanging: I think, I feel and I want?

When do you resort to the "we" power play and generalize on the collective instead of owning your own personal thoughts, feelings and desires?

14. *Humor*: When a meeting gets serious and the air is thick with conflict, it takes a certain skill and art to introduce some humor that can bring relief to the present situation. Humor misused at the wrong

time or with the wrong intention can derail a group from its attempt to break through the tension and discover resolution. Humor can be helpful if what is said invites the whole group to take a deep breath and change gears for just a moment. Humor can misfire if the joke is aimed at one person or seen as an avoidance tactic.

Do you have the skills to interject humor appropriately with your staff or parish leadership when a meeting gets serious or stuck in conflict?

15. *A shared vocabulary*: This could be a chapter unto itself. A significant point of reference that helps a group get unstuck from unresolved conflict is the clarification of terms and definitions. It never ceases to amaze me what people understand about commonly used church lingo and how badly church-related vocabulary can be misused. Here is a simple test for your staff, volunteers and leadership councils. Give them the list of terms below and have them write their definitions and applications to church work. After each person has had a chance to complete their personal definitions, compare definitions and applications as a group. If you find that most of your staff, volunteers or leadership councils have a common language and understanding of its applications, these groups most likely work well in conflict resolution and team building, while honoring the differences among their membership.

- Confidential
- Privileged information
- Private
- Secret
- Professional consultation
- Collaboration
- Consensus
- The seal of the confessional
- Mandatory reporting
- Sexual misconduct
- Dual relationships
- Triangulating communication
- Gossip
- Defamation of character
- Child abuse
- Elderly abuse

- Sexual abuse
- Stewardship
- Discernment
- Pastoral
- Pastoral care
- Spiritual direction
- Inner healing
- Counseling or psychotherapy—includes child, family, marriage, and alcohol/drug addiction specialties
- Church membership
- Social outreach services
- Ministry: Who can and when?
- Sacramental ministry: Who can and when?
- Preaching: Who can and when?
- Teaching: Who can and when?

Additional Resources

Consult the bibliography for complete publishing information on the following titles:

Tannen, Deborah. *Talking from 9 to 5.*
———. *That's Not What I Meant: How Conversational Style Makes or Breaks Relationships.*
———. *You Just Don't Understand: Women and Men in Conversation.*

Chapter 2
Rituals of Affection, and Internal and External Boundaries

Pastoral ministry can create an intimate exchange between the professional provider and those they serve. With skills of empathy, attending, listening and a nurturing presence, the pastor can be perceived as a helpful professional, an effective care provider, a loving servant, a best and only friend, and the one and only person who has ever cared for the recipient in such an intimate way. He who has title has the responsibility. This means that the provider, caring for another, has the responsibility to maintain both personal and professional boundaries. As the person in charge of giving, you are also responsible to manage the overlapping that occurs between a friendly relationship and someone who, after benefiting from your assistance, may consider you his/her best friend.

Anyone in the caring and helping ministry has most likely experienced the premature affections offered when they have cared for someone who has been beaten down by poor health, personal crises, family tragedy or loss of a loved one. The intimacy and vulnerability experienced between the care provider and the recipient is not mutual. Even though the recipient may imagine a reciprocal relationship, the provider has responsibility to maintain both personal and professional boundaries so as to protect the integrity of the caring relationship.

Imagine the last time you were really sick or recovering from some tragic life event. Remember how you struggled to make simple decisions? Managing daily activities seemed to evade your abilities. There may have been a constant fog that hung like a curtain between your mind's desire to get things done and your inability to accomplish them. Remember how grateful you were when someone came and

16

lightened your workload? The feelings of gratitude evolved into sensations of relief. The uplifting relief may have become feelings of deep gratitude and affection. The more dependent you became on the one who helped you, the more vulnerable you became.

Then there was that turning point when strong emotions of connection erupted and you realized that your gratitude had turned into feelings of safety and trust. What would have happened to me without so and so? How could I have ever gotten through this life event without so and so? The veil of dependency tends to bias the reality of what the helper and recipient perceive. In the end, it is the responsibility of the helper, the pastor, the pastoral leader to maintain effective and adaptable boundaries, assuring that whatever care is given comes with no strings attached.

Henry Cloud and John Townsend, in their book *Boundaries*, remind us, "…boundaries aren't inherited. They are built. To be the truth-telling, responsible, free, and loving people God wants us to be we need to learn limits from childhood on. Boundary development is an ongoing process, yet its most critical stages are in our very early years, where our character is formed."[1] This fact is mentioned in my book *Fathering the Next Generation: Men Mentoring Men*; our fathers help build the containers that provide us with measurement and proportion. Without our fathers' containers we have boys and girls without the adult life skills to manage, set limits, create boundaries, defend, maintain healthy competition, provide for themselves and develop the ability to say no when confronted with peer pressure, commercials and other influences that invite a violation of values and morals.[2]

Boundaries are those invisible fences that we create to protect us from infiltration of others who may want us to live, act and believe contrary to our personal beliefs and values. If you want to see a boundary in action, notice the physical and emotional space kept between yourself and others. How much physical and emotional distance do you maintain between coworkers, or your employer versus your family or close friends? The application of a boundary and its usage will measure the amount and frequency of self-disclosure, emotional demonstration, revealing thoughts and rituals of affection.

The list of actual boundaries cannot be exhausted. Some boundary descriptions will be mentioned in this chapter with the hope that the reader will evaluate how these boundaries fit his/her pastoral situation. I offer a few examples of some boundary demonstrations to illustrate how boundaries ebb and flow. The evolution of boundary development occurs throughout the life of the person, and is shaped and formed by social, peer, family and work relationships, as well as cultural and religious affiliations.

Some Examples

I was asked to provide the opening prayer for a confirmation retreat for teenagers who were between fifteen and sixteen years of age. On Friday night, at the retreat kick-off, I noticed that a few of the teenagers sat with their boyfriends or girlfriends, and were holding hands and making physical contact by touching knees and elbows. Then the rest of the group was clearly divided, with the girls sitting on the left and the boys sitting on the right. I came back on Sunday afternoon to celebrate the closing mass. What I saw was one mass body, with arms and legs crisscrossing and little or no physical space between any of the retreatants.

The retreat experience melted the emotional and physical boundaries and created a sense of safety that reduced the initial feelings of unfamiliarity. Through faith sharing, storytelling, small group activities, eating and praying together, making banners, laughing and crying throughout the whole weekend, the physical demonstrations of closeness and proximity achieved suggested that these teenagers realized, "We are the body of Christ and we are no longer strangers to one another." At the "kiss of peace" I was moved by the inclusivity among the high-status boys and girls and low-status boys and girls reaching out to greet one another with gestures of affection, hospitality and equality.

Here is another example of how a catastrophic event can break down social boundaries and family rituals of affection. I met a woman, Agnes, who tells the story that she was uninformed about the impending hurricane. She stayed in her townhouse while most of the city was vacated. The flooding came quickly, as she recalls. She got to the second floor of her home and realized that she made a terrible choice not to leave the city. A man in a boat came floating by her second-floor bedroom window and helped her into his boat. She recalls him hugging and holding her, reassuring her that she would be safe. As they went about helping others from their homes into the boat, Agnes began to offer each rescued person a hug and reassured him or her that they would be safe. As they made their way to safety, Agnes helped the others onto a landing site. She found herself hugging, holding and encouraging those who were still crying and frightened that all would be well.

A day later, while recovering from her tragic experience, men, women and children would find their way to Agnes, and she would offer hugs, holding them and reassuring them that all would be well. A week later, one of the FEMA supervisors asked Agnes if she would come to another FEMA center and help comfort those who were in serious distress. Agnes was amazed that this FEMA supervisor would be asking a middle-aged, African American to help with a multicultural community of men, women and children. The FEMA supervisor noticed how comfortable Agnes was working with all kinds of people, and he assumed she was some kind of professional care provider. Agnes declares, "I have never been married. I have no children. I have spent most of my life not trusting anyone and I don't like anyone touching me. Yet, here I am holding and hugging strangers who find me useful and helpful. Take me where you need me and let's get to work."

Family Rituals of Affection

Family rituals of affection like hugging, kissing, hand shaking, physical closeness and gestures of fondness are particular to each family shaped and influenced by cultural and religious rules. Each pastor and pastoral leader demonstrates rituals of affection that are fine-tuned by their particular church's culture or multiple cultures. The ultimate question I have heard from pastors, counselors, doctors, lawyers and other helping professionals is, "To hug or not to hug?" That is a chronic question that has to be dealt with in prudence and pastoral sensitivity.

It has been my experience that an Asian community offers a bow as a sign of respect and acknowledgment. While a strong, firm handshake is a typical gesture of welcome and hospitality from a farmer or rancher, a kiss on the cheek or a hug can mean the same for many Europeans. Each culture shapes and forms how we make contact and demonstrate our rituals of affection.

Checklist to Evaluate Your Rituals of Affection

Which rituals have you embraced?

Which rituals would you demonstrate with family, children, among friends, with church staff, volunteers and church members?

- A smile
- A smile with a wink of an eye
- A nod of the head
- A bow toward the other person
- Direct eye contact
- A gentle handshake—sometimes only touching fingers
- A firm and strong handshake
- A handshake using your free hand to cover the other person's hand
- A handshake with one hand while you hug with one arm around the back
- A hand on someone's shoulder
- Holding a person's face with both hands
- Wiping away a tear with your hand
- A hug using both hands around the back
- A quick kiss on the cheek with a hug
- A quick kiss on the cheek
- A hug with both hands around the person's back while holding them
- A hug with both hands around the person's back while holding and squeezing them
- A kiss on the lips
- A kiss on the upper side of the hand
- A kiss on the neck before you hug the person
- Keeping your arm around a person's shoulder after you have greeted them
- Keeping your arm around the waist of the person you have greeted
- Walking while holding hands
- Having someone sit on your lap
- Having someone sit right next to you allowing for arm and leg contact

- Having someone sit next to you with his or her arm around your neck
- Giving a gift with a note
- Giving a gift with a note of affection
- Giving an expensive gift with a note of significant affection

Rituals of affection are used to demonstrate intimacy, closeness, vulnerability, safety and trust. Those rituals demonstrated in the public forum can lock a person into repeating such a gesture to others. One pastor explained to me that the prior pastor started to invite the children up during the regular offertory, and after the children donated their "coins for kids," a few children would run up to the pastor and hug him. In time, other children stood in line for a hug until this "hugging time" with the pastor went from a simple five to seven minutes to twenty-five to thirty-five minutes. To hug or not to hug—especially in the public forum. Once you make a public display of affection, whom do you deny access to the ritual without offending or discriminating?

Defining Boundaries

Ask yourself, have you defined your workplace boundaries and professional boundaries, and do they help you accomplish healthy workplace relationships? Healthy boundaries keep things out and keep things in, depending on their purpose. Another image I like to use to describe a boundary is the purpose of a screen window. The screen on a window allows for air to come through but keeps most of the bugs out. If you were in the Caribbean, you would find that screening quickly rusts and rots. Instead of tight, woven screen, mosquito netting encircles your bed so that the tightness of the weave is denser than standard screening and thus keeps the smaller insects out, especially mosquitoes.

Also, in many of the Caribbean Islands, windows do not have screening or mosquito netting. Instead you will find a heavier fence material that is used to keep the birds out yet not dense enough to keep the flies and mosquitoes out.

Boundaries come in all sizes and shapes. What you want to keep inside or keep outside will shape and determine the density of your boundary. Also, the density and durability of your boundary determine its effectiveness. Through life experiences, especially painful moments, boundaries are tested. When we have adjusted the boundary to get what we want, it usually becomes the template for future applications.

Teenagers need to learn peer boundaries so that they can defend their choices for morality and ethics and keep others from pressuring them into doing something they really do not believe in or would not want to do. This is called "boundary power" or "ego stamina." Only through the practice of success and failure do young people learn how to defend and build strong boundaries. Developing strong boundaries helps manage choices and contributes to healthy young Christians in the making.

Words like *perseverance, stamina, discipline, inner strength, focus* and *concentration* address the inner mechanisms needed to manage boundaries. Without self-esteem and ego differentiation, no boundary in the world will help a person avoid becoming influenced by the last commercial seen or doing whatever friends say without any reference to consequences. Ego stamina (or call it moral or religious stamina) comes from inner strength, like a muscle that needs to be exercised and developed.

The primary exercise in developing ego stamina is "choice making." When parents provide choices for their children, the development of ego stamina is put into effect. When a child makes a good choice, positive consequences occur. When bad choices are made, bad consequences occur. Options provided are the raw materials to offer adults-in-the-making. Their ego stamina becomes strong through choice making.

Tell children what they can and can't do and you keep them powerless and weak. Tell adults what they can and can't do and they feel debased and disempowered. Good leadership, like effective parenting, provides options and directions. Choice making builds Christian leaders. Christian leaders come to realize they have power to make either good or bad choices. Both are choices that will be experienced. The skilled Christian leader realizes early on that lessons learned from bad choices can become moments of profound wisdom.

Some Boundary Examples

I prefer to address boundaries as internal and external. How do you know your particular boundary is working? When your choice to keep something in or keep something out is accomplished and you achieve your personal expectation, that's when you know that your boundary is developed and working effectively.

Internal Boundaries

1. *Setting limits*: Can you establish how much, how often, when to delay, when to avoid and when to keep to your committed goal(s)? This is one of the most basic life skills needed to develop other boundary skills. Setting limits teaches measurement and proportion to our choices and helps us realize amounts, value and quantity.

2. *Emotional boundaries*: Are you able to reveal feelings or emotions when you believe that they express what you want to express? Those who suffer from frozen feelings find it impossible to disclose them anytime, anywhere, with any one.

3. *Self-affirmation boundaries*: "I am wonderfully, beautifully made in God's image and likeness." Say this out loud to yourself three times. Then repeat this affirmation three times with a family member or close friend. When speaking well of our personal worth and value, self-esteem expands and generates a release of dopamine (the happy hormone) and contributes to our overall well-being and health.

4. *Intellectual boundaries*: This includes our habit thought patterns, vocabulary words and phrases that have become familiar to us. Each person develops a limited vocabulary and will discover early on in life that another person can use the same vocabulary and have a different meaning and significance. The capacities to clearly communicate what one thinks, independent of another's approval, suggest a person who has achieved autonomy, inner confidence and self-value. The ability to say, "I don't know," "show me" or "teach me" reflects a capacity to learn and grow in knowledge. Taking time to read, study, attend workshops and retreats and be mentored by another contributes to our collection of insights and intellect. The additional information helps us become more adaptable when an unknown experience confronts our understanding. "When the student is ready, the teacher will appear."

5. *Spiritual boundaries*: What prayer posture helps you become most present to God while at prayer? Some of our great mystics share that their best prayer occurs while walking in the woods; laying on a bed; kneeling in front of an icon or holy image; camping under the stars; living in a cave or hermitage; climbing trees or sitting quietly in

a church; or completing a pilgrimage. Spiritual boundaries include images of God, styles of prayer and worship such as a charismatic prayer meeting or the solitude of adoration before the Blessed Sacrament. The spiritual disciplines we find helpful in achieving union with God add to our repertoire of spiritual boundaries. Our menu of prayer forms, gestures at worship, music choices, religious beliefs and how we share them with others will determine who we pray with, how often and whether or not we become faithful members of a church or congregation.

6. *Values and beliefs boundaries*: The basic premise to faith and moral development assumes that our mothers and fathers, our family and culture, and our religious community have contributed to our understanding of simple tasks such as: knowing right from wrong, good from bad; living the Ten Commandments; following the basic teachings of Jesus Christ; internalizing the spiritual and corporal works of mercy, and accepting the call to live honestly, do good deeds and love our neighbor as ourselves. When teaching children through storytelling and letting the moral question hang without a quick answer, I am amazed at the depth of theology that children can access. Values, attitudes and beliefs about a power that is greater than self comes naturally to children. Encouraging children to listen to the good within and act on the desire to love and serve will nurture this particular boundary. The second best way to help children develop this boundary is to watch their parents and other family members demonstrate through good deeds and acts of charity their values and beliefs. Such demonstrations make a permanent mark on the next generation.

7. *Communication boundaries*: This particular boundary has many levels and compartments. Some of these include: the volume of your voice; speaking clearly; using intonation and inflection, local jargon, slang and innuendoes; direct or indirect eye contact; how closely you stand when speaking to another; the use of personal or professional, formal or informal communication strategies. Being introverted versus extraverted can also bias how you communicate. The extravert seems to be more comfortable in a large crowd using many words to make a point. On the other hand, the introvert feels more comfortable with just a few close friends and shares sparingly of thoughts and feelings, using fewer words. Some people are inclusive in their first contact with another and encourage shared communication and information. Another person may

be more hesitant and cautious and rely upon objective and informal information, testing the dynamics of the communication exchange before moving into something more personal and informal. When you are with friends do you have communication boundaries that help you withhold personal and confidential information? If your communication boundaries are weak and permeable you may find yourself revealing information that violates your family's, spouse's or best friend's expectations of personal or privileged information.

The following are some "red flags" for poor communication boundaries:

- Speaks quickly and does not invite others to talk
- Interrupts while another person is speaking
- Completes another person's sentence
- Talks over another person and does not let the other person complete his/her thought or sharing
- Looks preoccupied or does other tasks rather than making eye contact and looking attentive to the speaker
- Shouts and yells so as to create dominance in the conversation
- Uses moral imperatives so as to restrict open and honest communication: You should, ought to, could, must, have to, never, ever, always…
- Whispers or speaks so softly the person can not be heard
- Does not maintain eye contact (unless culturally typical)
- Speaks with apology
- Repeats what has already been said
- Uses physical gestures like pounding fists on a table, kicking a chair, throwing objects, pointing a finger at the person, and pacing
- Walks away before a mutual agreement to pause or end the conversation
- Gives ultimatums or threats to coerce the person into agreement
- Quotes others, books, famous people to defend a belief and manipulate a person into submission
- Ignories a person who is trying to speak
- Answers the phone while in the middle of a conversation

- Watches television or looks at the computer monitor when a person is trying to speak
- Refuses to give the time and energy to discuss differences in perception
- Resorts to blaming, accusing, generalizing (it's all your fault), avoiding any personal responsibility for the problem, cursing and using vulgar language, telling sexual jokes or suggesting sexual gender inferiority (you can't help but not understand because you are a man)
- Uses a top dog—bottom dog strategy (you are only an employee—you don't understand the dynamics of being a supervisor)

External Boundaries That Are Worth Considering: Are They Working Well for You?

a. Workplace boundaries
b. Body-awareness boundaries
c. Power and control boundaries
d. Environmental boundaries
e. Touch boundaries
f. Space boundaries
g. Sound boundaries
h. Visual boundaries

Additional Resources

Consult the bibliography for complete publishing information on the following titles:

Cloud, Henry, and John Townsend. *Boundaries*.
————. *Setting Boundaries with Your Adult Children*.

Chapter 3
How to Create a Hostile Work Environment in Ten Easy Steps

1. *Discrimination*: any behavior, vocabulary, treatment or attitude toward another that suggests a diminution, degradation or prejudice of a person because of race, gender, culture, age, sexual preference, marital status, religious beliefs and practices, or physical or mental limitations.

2. *Sexual Harassment*: "the sexualization of an instrumental relationship through the introduction or imposition of sexist or sexual remarks, requests or requirements in the context of a formal power differential. Harassment can also occur where no such formal power differential exists, if the behavior is unwanted by, or offensive to, the woman (man). Instances of harassment can be classified into the following general categories: gender harassment, seductive behavior, solicitation of sexual activity by promise of reward or threat of punishment, and sexual imposition or assault."[1]

3. *Gender Harassment*: consists of generalized sexist remarks and behavior not designed to elicit sexual cooperation, but rather to convey insulting, degrading or sexist attitudes about women (men) or about lesbians and gays.[2]

4. *Workplace Harassment*: When an employee feels unsafe and unwelcome and his/her work performance is limited or interrupted because of the actions of another, the foundation for workplace harassment has begun. If an employee has experiences of being offended by the words and actions of others, these actions need to be noticed and documented by another person. If the employee has been treated in such a way that he/she has been humiliated in front of others, addressed

27

with derogatory remarks, offended by the actions or words of another employee or employer, experienced selective treatment aimed exclusively at the employee, unreasonably interfering with work performance, or has perceived gestures or words as offensive or demeaning, workplace harassment is at hand.

5. *Cultural Harassment*: Most of our Christian churches are experiencing the melting pot of a multicultural emergence. Sensitivity to the pastoral needs and inclusion of the various ways people like to affiliate is a minimum requirement for multicultural churches. I was a consultant with a church in Texas that has documented serving over forty different cultures and nationalities within their church membership. I was amazed at this community's inclusivity, demonstrated by the international food festival it sponsors each year and the arts and crafts fair it encourages. At this event church members display the arts and crafts particular to their culture and nation.

Cultural harassment usually takes the forms of prejudice, ignorance or misunderstanding of cultural innuendoes; impatience, especially with language barriers and differing expectations of the pastor and requirements for sacramental preparations; and annoyance and disregard for customs particular to a culture.

Let's say that a new pastor comes to a church and is informed that on Holy Saturday many of the families bring a basket of food to be blessed. Some of the blessed food is donated to the local soup kitchen for their Easter Sunday breakfast and lunch. The new pastor, unfamiliar with this custom, sees no value in offering his presence and time. When a hundred families show up at 9:00 a.m. for their expected blessing of food, the receptionist reads a note to the attending church members informing them that such a custom of blessing of food holds no value to the pastor and that he will not participate in any way. Is this cultural harassment? Not in the strict sense. This is insensitivity to a custom shared by church families that complimented their preparations for the Easter celebrations and their contributions to feeding the poor. Customs, cultural traditions and practices, tribal rituals and unique expressions that embody both family and culture need to be carefully handled with pastoral sensitivity and education for both the pastor and those served.

6. *Academic Harassment*: "An intimidating, hostile or offensive working or learning environment" indicates conditions typical of aca-

demic harassment.[3] The National Advisory Council on Women's Educational Programs has defined academic sexual harassment as the use of authority to emphasize the sexuality or sexual identity of the student in a manner that prevents or impairs that student's full enjoyment of educational benefits, climate or opportunities."[4]

7. *Peer or Group Harassment*: When two or more people unite to harass an individual through intimidation, verbal assaults, vulgarity, slang, sexually derogatory remarks or verbal sexual advances, peer and/or group harassment has been committed. Peer harassment occurs in all types of academic and business settings—large and small, private and public. Peer harassment creates an environment that makes education and work less than equal for women and men.[5] Examples of group harassment include: scoping—rating a (man) woman's attractiveness on a scale from one to ten; yelling, whistling and shouting obscenities at women who walk by fraternity houses or other campus sites; intimidating a woman by surrounding her, demanding that she expose her breasts and not allowing her to leave until she complies; creating a disturbance outside of women's residence halls; vandalizing sororities; harassing women who support women's rights; and, finally, date rape.[6]

The most unfortunate cases of this type of harassment occur on school playgrounds or in high school showers. The school bully can act out his or her violations independent of a supportive group of followers, but the real pathological bully gathers others to aid in his or her attacks on boys and girls or men and women who are perceived as vulnerable, unusual or nonconforming. When the group begins to mock, name call and verbally intimidate, all members involved are equally responsible for harming the victim.

8. *Verbal Abuse and Physical Gestures of Intimidation*: This type of harassment includes derogatory remarks, verbal assaults, using sexual jokes or sexual imagery to embarrass or demean, name calling, cursing, raging, yelling, intimidating through physical gestures, using volatile and violent words, threatening to do harm, infiltrating another person's social space, finger pointing, shaking a fist at another or making hand or arm gestures that suggest vulgarity or violence.

9. *Religious and Spiritual Abuse and Harassment*: This is more difficult to describe and even more difficult to measure due to the variety of religious traditions and practices throughout the world. I will keep the definition of religious and spiritual abuse and/or harassment to

behaviors that can be offensive and harmful. Religious and spiritual abuse occurs when religious and spiritual practices exclude personal choice and respect of free will. When religious disciplines are used to control a person, create fear, shame, guilt and terror, religious abuse abounds. When religious or spiritual practices alienate others from common sense, create spiritual arrogance, encourage attitudes that "we" are better than "them," a cascade of harm will feed division, prejudice and entitlement and ultimately form hardened hearts. The capacity to question and ponder our faith and spiritual encounters validates religious maturity and spiritual growth. Promoting and demanding blind obedience and unquestionable submission or establishing spiritual disciplines that harm physical and mental health and well-being not only alienate people from their family, friends and hospitality, but also constitutes evidence of a pathological use of religion and spirituality.

The following story exemplifies poor judgment about illustrating religious and spiritual abuse and harassment.

Particular denominations define themselves by how they worship and how they share prayer rituals. When leading a parish mission to an all African American southern Catholic congregation, I invited a family who participated in one of our lay leadership training programs at the Mercy Center in Colorado Springs, Colorado, to attend. While I presided and gave the sermon, the congregation offered spontaneous praise, hands lifted up, clapping to the music, and throughout my sermon offered spontaneous responses such as "Praise the Lord!" and "Alleluia!" My charismatic background helped me appreciate the exchange between the congregation and myself. My invited guests were reduced to shock and terror. I did not realize that they had no experience of charismatic prayer and praise. While at dinner that night, I apologized and tried to catechize them about praise, charismatic music and gestures of worship typical to what they experienced. On my part, it was an error in judgment.

Honoring the differences in religious and spiritual practices is a sign of a mature Christian. Hospitality is the hallmark of God's presence among us. Polarizing a community with mandates to pray one way or another is abusive use of power in leadership and creates a foundation for religious arrogance and persecution. Whether a person is invited to attend a Tridentine mass or a Life Teen mass, centering prayer or a charismatic prayer group, a weekend hermitage of solitude and silence or a college Encounter Christ weekend, the difference between a religious experience and religious abuse is the emphasis on "choice." Inviting others to stretch their comfort zone can be provocative and exhilarating. When free-will choice making is replaced by applied coercion, oppression, guilt, shame and fear of consequences, a spiritual paralysis binds the opportunity for Christian maturity and movement toward holiness.

10. *Coworker Harassment*: This is becoming a complicated matter for employers and corporations around the world. Most people would acknowledge that their social network and some of their close friends have come mainly through associations in the workplace. The problem emerges when conflict in personal relationships overlaps into the workplace. When unwarranted and unwanted relational gestures are made between employees, it is the job of the person feeling harassed to report such matters to their employer. Once reported, sanctions and documentation must take place immediately. This usually begins with an interview so that perceptions can be assessed and agreements made between the two parties involved. However, it has been documented that even after some employees have registered their perceptions and the initial intervention has been completed, the coworker harassment continues. Coworker harassment may include: inappropriate e-mails, letters and cards; repeated phone calls and hang-ups at home; repeated invitations to social activities; stalking and staring; driving by the employee's home or following the employee to social events; and leaving anonymous letters and gifts, some of which may be vulgar, threatening or sexual in nature. When coworker harassment continues outside the workplace, additional resources need to be secured. This may involve making a formal report to the local police, securing a restraining order and asking friends and family to be with you when entering and leaving your workplace, and upon entering and leaving your home. Other safety precautions may be necessary. At this point, it would be best to seek professional consultation in order to feel confident about how you protect yourself and your family from unwanted harassment.

Recommended Reading to Understand Related Employment Laws and Regulations

Civil Rights Act of 1866
Civil Rights Act of 1964
Equal Employment Opportunity Act
Age Discrimination in Employment Act of 1967
Older Workers Benefit Protection Act
Immigration Reform and Control Act
Equal Pay Act
Uniformed Services Employment and Reemployment Act
Vocational Rehabilitation and Other Rehabilitation Services of 1973
Americans with Disabilities Act of 1990
Americans with Disabilities Act—Amendment Act of 2009
Vietnam Era Veterans Readjustment Assistance Act of 1974
Sarbanes-Oxley Act (Whistleblower Protection)
Genetic Information Nondiscrimination Act
Pregnancy Discrimination Act
Nursing Mothers Workplace Law
Domestic Violence Victims Leave
Marital Status Discrimnation Laws
Workers' Compensation Laws
National Labor Relations Act

Additional Resources

Consult the bibliography for complete publishing information on the following titles:

Paludi, Michele A., and Richard B. Barickman. *Academic and Workplace Sexual Harassment.*
Thomas, Oliver. *10 Things Your Minister Wants to Tell You But Can't Because He Needs the Job.*

Chapter 4
Dual Relationships and the Continuum of Social Relationships

For those who work in a church job, dual relationships can be minimized and managed well. However, they cannot be avoided.

What is a dual relationship? A dual relationship is the overlapping of roles and relationships between employer and employee or pastor and church member. Those with title and position who move from a professional and unequal relationship to behaviors that suggest a personal and mutual relationship create and sustain a dual relationship.

Dual relationships are rarely a clear-cut matter for church ministers. Often, judgment calls and the careful application of ethical codes to specific situations are needed. Dual relationships are fraught with complexities and ambiguities. They can be problematic along a number of dimensions: (1) they are pervasive, (2) they can be difficult to recognize, (3) they are sometime unavoidable, (4) they can be very harmful but not always harmful and (5) they are the subject of conflicting advice from expert sources.[1]

As helping professionals, we enter into a dual relationship whenever we have another, significantly different relationship with one of our clients, students or supervisees. When we play dual roles, the potential exists for a conflict of interest and for exploiting those who seek our help.[2]

Today there is clear agreement that sexual dual relationships are unethical, and prohibitions against them have been codified into ethical standards and law.[3]

Kenneth S. Pope has provided a clear and comprehensive picture of the harm done to clients because of sexual relationships with their

33

therapists. These harmful consequences parallel what happens when a pastor or parish leader crosses the professional boundaries and encourages a sexual relationship with those he or she serves. Ten general aspects commonly associated with the syndrome are ambivalence, guilt, emptiness and isolation, identity/boundary/role confusion, sexual confusion, impaired ability to trust, emotional liability, suppressed rage, cognitive dysfunction and increased suicidal risk.[4]

Virtually all professional codes of ethics prohibit sexual intimacies with clients and declare that such a relationship is unethical.

Here are two situations that involve a dual relationship. Consider how you would counsel those involved?

1. How would you counsel a single male pastor who believes that his love for another single female staff member is ready to evolve into a consecrated relationship?
2. How would you counsel a single female pastor who believes that her love for a single male church member is ready to evolve into a consecrated relationship?

Options for Case 1

A. Have both the pastor and staff member resign from their jobs and find employment outside the church so that their future relationship would not put either of them in question of a dual relationship.
B. Have the pastor or the staff member resign and develop their relationship outside of their church membership.
C. Invite the pastor to consider terminating his growing relationship with the staff member because it is an obvious dual relationship and he has breached his professional responsibilities by encouraging this dual relationship.
D. What's so wrong with two single people falling in love and moving into a consecrated relationship?

Options for Case 2

A. Have the pastor resign from her job and find employment outside the church so that her future relationship would not put her in question of a dual relationship.

B. Have the church member relocate to another church and develop the relationship outside of his present church membership.

C. Invite the pastor to consider terminating her growing relationship with the church member because it is an obvious dual relationship and she has breached her professional responsibilities by encouraging this dual relationship.

D. What's so wrong with two single people falling in love and moving into a consecrated relationship?

What other options would you consider for either case?

These examples, of course, would exclude any man ordained in the Roman Catholic Church unless the ordained priest has made a clear discernment to leave priestly ministry. Those men I have worked with who have made the transition from ordained ministry to married life have done so successfully because they were prudent, patient and prayerfully considered their transition without much fanfare and publicity.

The person with title, position and authority has the responsibility for managing a professional relationship in all matters pertaining to his or her employees. An effective pastor creates a friendly and caring environment that encourages personal and pastoral dynamics in the workplace. Although the professional relationship may involve a caring, supportive and a pastoral relationship that reflects the best qualities of a good friendship, it is not a friendship. The person responsible for communicating the professional relationship and clarifying the difference between personal and professional is the person with title, position and authority.

This means that the pastor has a professional relationship with employees. The pastor has a professional relationship with church volunteers and church members. In addition, the pastor may have a personal relationship with a few select church members.

Pastors and church staff and volunteers work within the particular definition of what a dual relationship includes. That is why pastors and church staff workers need to carefully manage and work within the reality that dual relationships happen. Each church leader needs to take the first step and be proactive in managing the consequences of church dual relationships.

Some Dual Relationships That Need to Be Avoided

The pastor has an administrative and/or evaluative relationship with an employee who seeks personal or marital counseling from the pastor.

A church employee wants to discuss personnel problems with the pastor within the seal of the confessional.

A church employee becomes a social friend with the pastor. The pastor now has impaired objectivity and professional judgment as to the employee's work performance.

A church staff member develops an exclusive working relationship with a church volunteer. Other volunteers are feeling excluded and unappreciated, and the church staff member is too busy to make time to meet their needs for information and direction.

The church pastor needs to clarify and communicate what belongs to the work relationship and what belongs in the personal relationship. The following practices are essential to this balance:

- Creating boundaries that keep the work at work.
- Avoiding public displays of privilege or honor to friends in the workplace.
- Keeping personal phone calls and correspondence out of the workplace.
- Teaching your friends about the need for social privacy and maintaining propriety when in shared social situations like a church picnic, festival or dinner.
- Friends joining the pastor for a parish social event must remember that the pastor's time belongs to all the church members—not to one exclusive person.

Some Examples of Dual Relationships

The director of religious education, Mrs. Brown, has two part-time employees, Debra and Janet. Mrs. Brown becomes emotionally

36

enmeshed and overinvolved in Debra's impending divorce. Mrs. Brown spends hours per week coaching her employee and providing hours of time to listen to Debra's painful experiences. There are many complaints from those parents who feel that Debra cannot do her job and has shortchanged both students and parents from experiencing a quality sacramental preparation program. The pastor asks that Mrs. Brown inform Debra that either improvement in her job performance must occur quickly or someone else may have to take over her job. Mrs. Brown explains this to Debra, who feels betrayed by Mrs. Brown because she thought they were friends due to all the extra time Mrs. Brown afforded Debra. Debra perceived that the pastoral care and support given by Mrs. Brown were gestures of friendship. Debra does not hear the pastor or parents' concerns about her poor job performance. She quits her job feeling betrayed by Mrs. Brown.

The pastor of St. Bernard's Church relies on volunteers to help with his growing congregation. There are three married couples that have become integral to many of the ongoing service projects and church ministries. All three couples have known one another for years and have shared a long-term friendship with one another. Over time one couple, Mr. and Mrs. Johnson, seem to have become more empathetic and connect with the pastor on a more personal level than the others.

The pastor finds he is spending more time at the Johnson family home and enjoys his time with Mr. and Mrs. Johnson and their two teenage boys. The extra time and the personal gestures of affection shared between the pastor and the Johnson couple have become apparent to the other couples and church members. The other two families are feeling left out and second-best, so they begin to withdraw their availability of both time and talent. Mr. and Mrs. Johnson are noticing the negative vibes from their couple friends and take great offense at the petty jealousy among them.

Within a few months, the Johnsons are excluded from the usual Memorial Day gathering and the July Fourth picnic that have been celebrated together with the other couples' friends and family. The Johnson boys are told that they are not welcome to come and play with their friends and come home in tears. The pastor polarizes the parish by including in his Sunday sermon inferences of the jealousy, alienation and hurtful criticisms going on between the Johnson family and the other couples. Immediately after the pastor's sermon, the other two couples, along with some of their friends, leave St. Bernard's church.

Mrs. Parcel, the parish secretary, has been in her position for twenty years and has been a church member of Holy Spirit Church for over thirty years. She is well known throughout the church membership as someone who is competent, dependable and thorough. Mr. Stone, the chairman of the buildings and grounds committee, has been actively engaged in researching and developing the plans for the new addition to the church. Over the last five years, Mr. Stone has worked with the many church and diocesan committees to secure the blueprints, the architectural drawings and the needed permits to begin the construction on the church addition. Mr. Stone has relied on Mrs. Parcel to keep the pastor and church members informed about each stage of the overall project and to publish related information in the Sunday bulletin. Mr. Stone has enjoyed both lunch and dinner with Mrs. Parcel so that they could exchange information and negotiate the best options for informing church members.

Mr. Stone, who works a full-time job, has found that lunchtime or dinnertime was the best arrangement he could make to keep Mrs. Parcel up-to-date on the overall building project. Sometimes the pastor would join them for a meal and share in the planning.

Mrs. Parcel's husband, Tony Parcel, is a well-known contractor and has put a bid on the overall construction project. The diocese requires at least three to five bids from various contractors. After each contractor has been interviewed and their proposal reviewed, the Buildings and Grounds Committee makes a recommendation to the diocese for the final approval on which contractor will receive the upcoming construction job. Tony Parcel's company does not receive the job.

Mr. Stone then noticed a significant change in personality and approachability in regard to Mrs. Parcel. She became cold, aloof and quick-tempered with Mr. Stone. Mrs. Parcel failed to pass on important messages to the pastor, did not return phone calls, forgot to publish information relating to the ongoing construction project and spoke badly about Mr. Stone and his competency in completing the church addition. Mr. Stone, who had volunteered all his time and effort, was no longer able to work with Mrs. Parcel. Mr. Stone then asked the pastor to step in and address Mrs. Parcel's change of behavior toward Mr.

Stone and the obvious sabotaging of disseminating information to both pastor and church members.

Examples of How a Dual Relationship Was Managed Well

Father James, the pastor of St. Elsewhere, becomes friends with a married couple, the Jacksons, who have three children. He is welcomed to drop by anytime for dinner or holidays and enjoy a good meal and some quality friendly family time. When the pastor greets the church members as they walk into the church building, people feel his warmth and genuine hospitality. When the Jacksons walk in, he is at ease to hug and kiss them like he would any of his own family members. The pastor has learned from past relationships that it is best not to have the Jackson family demand any more attention than those of the parish at large. He has also learned not to have the Jackson family serve on leadership councils so that he can keep parish business at the parish.

This pastor has learned that he values friendships and, because of his friends, he has been an effective pastor and a healthy human person. His priest friends and his own family know about his friendship with the Jackson family, and they can each acknowledge their hope and encouragement for Father James. He can talk about the importance of friends and family in his sermons, but does not mention the Jackson family by name. Keeping social boundaries and maintaining personal space is a sign of healthy ego identity.

Father James makes time to be with his "family friends" while maintaining other friendships. He has a personal rule that when he is with his "family friends" the whole family be present. He explained to Mr. and Mrs. Jackson that he would prefer not to come to the Jackson home if only Mrs. Jackson is at home. This does not suggest that he doesn't trust himself or Mrs. Jackson. Father James is aware of the power of rumors and gossip and wants to defend and protect the dignity of his friendship with the Jackson family.

Father Daniel has been friends with Allen since high school. He presided at Allen's wedding and over time has developed a friendly relationship with Allen's wife, Sue. Father Daniel and Allen like to go hiking and have spent many vacations together hiking throughout the

Rocky Mountains. Sue has been happy to see Allen take a week off and go hiking because it is something he loves to do, and it contributes to Allen's health and well-being. Allen and Sue move into Father Daniel's parish and begin to attend church and enroll their two children at the parish elementary school. Sue finds herself in a serious conflict with the first-grade teacher over some disciplinary procedure that involved Sue's daughter.

Sue contacts Father Daniel, who explains that school matters need to be taken through proper channels and refers her to the school principal. Sue is not pleased with the principal's response and again asks that Father Daniel step in on her behalf. Father Daniel suggests that again proper channels be exhausted and that Sue should meet with the principal, the first-grade teacher and the superintendent of schools. Sue agrees, and the outcome of that meeting does not meet up to Sue's expectations. Sue demands that Father Daniel take immediate steps to resolve her concerns. Father Daniel agrees to meet with Sue and Allen and asks that the principal and first-grade teacher come along for the discussion. Sue agrees.

The meeting takes place, and Sue demands that Father Daniel fire the first-grade teacher. Father Daniel tries to facilitate a discussion about Sue's concerns, but cannot get Sue to negotiate or agree upon some middle ground and move toward reconciliation. The meeting ends with Sue walking out cursing and threatening a lawsuit. Allen is left with obvious embarrassment and apologizes for his wife's behavior.

The next day Allen's two children are withdrawn from the parish school. Weeks after the meeting, Father Daniel gets a phone call from Allen saying that he cannot go on their planned hike this month. Father Daniel is very hurt by this and realizes that his hurt is shared in kind with Allen. Father Daniel realizes that his friendship with Allen cannot be saved; the marriage between Allen and Sue outweighs the friendship between Father Daniel and Allen.

In a dual relationship, pastors need to teach their friends how to be friends. Pastors and employees can rarely be friends. To do so opens them up to the potential for conflicts of interest and the power differential. The pastor has the power and authority to hire and fire. The employee does not.

Pastors can become friends with church volunteers and parish families with careful management and a standing awareness of the possible negative consequences.

Here is an example of an unfortunate situation that happened because a dual relationship with a parish family was poorly managed.

Father Ben befriended the parish secretary. The parish secretary, Mrs. Thomas, was the only full-time paid person on the parish staff. There was a part-time maintenance man, but the pastor and volunteers managed everything else. Father Ben was a first-time pastor working in a rural parish setting. Mr. and Mrs. Thomas had a standing invitation for Father Ben to come for dinner every Tuesday and Thursday evening. Father Ben felt good about his time with the Thomas family, and it gave him a chance to eat a meal with a family. Some of the neighbors had noticed that Father Ben was coming to the Thomas home twice a week. These neighbors, of course, were church members. Some of the ladies of the church began to comment to Mrs. Thomas that she had the pastor's ear and that she could speak on their behalf about some concerns they had about parish finances and the lack of effective parish programs for their children.

One particular night while at dinner, Mrs. Thomas brought up the concerns mentioned by the three ladies of the parish. Mr. Thomas and Father Ben made attempts to reassure Mrs. Thomas that she had no responsibility to speak on behalf of the concerned ladies. The ladies of the parish approached Mrs. Thomas the next day, and they became upset that she had not lobbied for their concerns. Mrs. Thomas again mentioned this to Father Ben while at their shared evening meal. Father Ben began to feel uncomfortable about the triangle communication among the ladies of the parish, Mrs. Thomas and himself.

Father Ben called the three ladies to his office and informed them that it is inappropriate for them to pressure Mrs. Thomas to be their spokesperson. If they had concerns, they knew they could come directly to him or speak to someone on the parish council and make suggestions on how best to resolve their concerns. During the conversation, one of the ladies mentioned that her concerns about the parish programs were less disconcerting concerting to her than the privileged relationship Father Ben had created with Mr. and Mrs. Thomas. This lady went on to say that there were rumors that Mrs. Thomas and Father Ben may be having an affair. Father Ben exploded! He rebuked this woman for her gossip and slander, and demanded that the three ladies immediately leave his office. Father Ben, at the next weekend masses, included in his homily the evils of gossip and slander, and that some people of the church had been sponsoring slanderous ideas about himself and Mrs. Thomas. The church membership became polarized. Father Ben's homily impacted the church membership like gasoline poured onto an open fire.

There were some church members who were appalled at what was suggested between Mrs. Thomas and Father Ben, while others thought it was suspicious that Father Ben would bring this to the attention of the entire church. Still others had become enthralled with the accusation against Father Ben and Mrs. Thomas. A few weeks later, Mrs. Thomas resigned as the parish secretary and began to attend a church twenty miles from her home. Father Ben no longer felt safe to share meals with the Thomas family. Rumors and accusations continued and, within three months, Father Ben requested a transfer to serve in another church.

Chapter 12 will explore the power of gossip and slander, and how to intervene in such matters. Chapter 7 will help explain the power of projections, including both infatuations and repulsions.

The Continuum of Social Relationships

Have you ever wondered about the variety of relationships that can be established throughout a lifetime? Personal relationships run the continuum from social acquaintance that may have been formed through work, social interests and recreation possibilities. Professional relationships are established because of services provided and resources that assume a trained, licensed and/or certified provider and/or a professional college degree. Each continuum of personal and professional relationships is important to distinguish so that the provider and the recipient do not create false expectations or unrealistic relationship demands. As you review the relationship continuum, where would you place your family, friends, coworkers and professional providers?

A professional relationship: This occurs between any professional provider and the person he or she serves. The relationship is created to serve the needs of the person he/she provides services for. This is an unequal relationship and may include intimate self-disclosure, deep trust and a short-term or long-term relationship. Such examples would include: pastor and church and school staff; manager and coworkers; teacher and student; doctor and patient; counselor and client; massage therapist and client, etcetera.

A professional relationship that is friendly yet formal: This occurs among providers who build a level of trust to accomplish their jobs. These relationships assume well-developed social skills and communication skills. The provider can set boundaries and limits while providing his/her skills or service.

A professional relationship that is friendly and informal: This type of relationship occurs in support groups, workshops and retreats, conferences and other learning opportunities, classroom settings, bible study, prayer groups and volunteer activities. Most people who serve in the helping professions provide this type of relationship so as to create a trusting and deferential level of interaction. Men and women trained in pastoral skills and the ability to create an enduring relationship usually serve as clergy, pastors, youth ministers and pastoral-care workers, especially those serving as chaplains. Interactions within such frameworks can be confusing to those who do not have a foundation for relationships, in particular, friendships. Those who are craving a relationship may misinterpret the empathetic skills of a provider as a gesture of friendship. People come together to contribute to an experience through active participation and engagement. The person leading or facilitating the experience will exchange personal information so that common interests build group cohesion and participation in the shared activities.

Employee–employer relationship: The leadership or management style of the employer will shape and form the employee-employer relationship. No matter how much trust and friendly feelings are exchanged between employer and employee, it always remains an unequal relationship. He who has the title has full responsibility. The employer is always in the power position.

Relationships with coworkers: Workplace intimacy can occur and is shaped by the amount of time and closeness of the work space shared, the exchange of work responsibilities and the need to network and communicate information that impacts job productivity. This type of intimacy looks a lot like a long-term friendship. The difference would be the depth of self-disclosure and the level of engagement with the coworker outside of the workplace. When people work eight hours a day, five days a week for two to twenty-five years, a profound sense of familiarity can be achieved. Talk time, shared tasks, compatibility and interaction will shape and determine the depth of friendliness, dependability and workplace familiarity. It is typical that when the work environment is no longer a common shared factor, the coworker relationship will diminish, if not expire all together.

Long-term relationships with coworkers: There is a bond achieved with long-term coworkers. It is typical at this level of relationship that coworkers have shared holidays, met each other's family and extended family, and socialized after work hours and on weekends.

Situational acquaintance: This may occur while your children attend after-school programs or sports and recreational activities. The social acquaintance typically occurs in some form of shared group activity.

Social acquaintance that includes shared recreation experiences: This type of relationship evolves the longer the shared recreation experience lasts. This occurs in bowling leagues, volleyball teams and other shared recreational and competitive sports.

A casual friend: This friendship is spontaneous and based on mutual convenience. Social plans made to include a casual friend do not determine the choice of the activity.

A social friend who shares in specific activities: This could include sharing in a recreational activity such as playing bridge with the same people over a prolonged period of time, going to the movies, sharing vacation experiences and playing board games or cards.

A long-term friend: Someone who has been involved in your life and has collected memories with you about your various life experiences. This person is usually known by your family and other friends. The commitment of time contributes to the value of this relationship.

A good friend: Someone who takes turns with you initiating activities and includes you in social activities that may involve other people. Each has a high level of dependability, a willingness to sacrifice for the other, and trusts and defers to their friend for shared advice and decision-making. Your family and other friends usually know this person.

A best friend: This relationship includes mutual self-disclosure, in-depth trust and intimacy, allowing for an exchange of power and control. Strong emotional attachment occurs, along with the sharing of time and resources.

A soul mate: Someone that has shared significant life experiences, resulting in a profound sense of knowing the other. Mutual interests, values, morals and religious beliefs intensify this relationship.

When sex becomes a part of any of the possible relationships, it can either deepen the relationship or elevate it to a more significant status in a person's life. Sexual activity can also create a demand that may not contribute to the maturation of a relationship. Instead, sex replaces what use to be the point of connection.

A sexual relationship in any professional situation is a violation of most professional codes of ethics. If sex is the starting point, a friendship may not be possible. Can friends ever be lovers? Can lovers ever return to the friendship level? Some have survived the transition while many suffer the causalities of becoming physically intimate before they secured a foundation for emotional intimacy.

Additional Resources

Consult the bibliography for complete publishing information on the following titles:

Finzel, Hans. *The Top Ten Mistakes Leaders Make*.
Herlihy, Barbara, and Gerald Corey. *Dual Relationships in Counseling*.
Keating, Charles J. *Dealing with Difficult People*.
Lamdin, Keith, and David Tilley. *Supporting New Ministers in the Local Church*.
Lutz, Robert R., and Bruce T. Taylor. *Surviving in Ministry*.
Ventura, Steve. *Start Right Stay Right*.

Chapter 5
Confidential, Privileged Information, Private-Internal Forum and Public-External Forum

In today's rapid information network, immediate news publications, international and national twenty-four-hour news reporting, e-mail, voice-mail, cell phones and snail-mail (post office mail), today's church leaders need a filter to help them separate the personal from the professional, internal forum from external forum, privileged information from confidential, and what must be reported to the law and what can be withheld from the public forum.

The best guidelines I can suggest are learning the definitions of each of the words that will be explored in this chapter. Your common sense is your best guide. Seek legal, canonical and corporate advice when you have doubts about managing information that could be volatile or condemning, that could jeopardize the health and well-being of another person or that could harm yourself, your church and your diocese.

> *Confidential* 1. Communicated in confidence; secret; hence, private; as, a confidential file (of documents) 3. Enjoying, or treated with, confidence....
> *Confidence* 5. Reliance upon another's secrecy and fidelity; as, to tell in confidence
> *Confidentiality* The withholding and keeping information from others[1]

Confidentiality is never absolute. If a pastor or parish leader is asked to keep information confidential, the first question to ask is "Why?" Matters of confidentiality usually involve some negative consequence if the information is shared. As a pastor or parish leader you may want to assess if the burden and responsibility of confidentiality is what you are offering to another.

Just as knowing the sequence to launch nuclear weapons would suggest limited access to those we trust to protect the greater good, so also in matters of gossip, second-hand information (e.g., "Keep this confidential, but did you know…") should be avoided at all costs.

Confidential records are never absolute. If you are required by the courts to provide related documents to a legal case, you had best do so with the advice of your lawyer.

Staff evaluations and staff personal records are considered *restricted information* because more than one person usually manages them. Restricted information suggests that only those preapproved may access personnel records, including salary and benefits.

Job descriptions are never confidential or restricted as a matter of privacy. There will be a chapter on the importance of job descriptions, and this information is best shared with all involved in a person's job responsibilities.

A church member comes to you and begins the conversation with, "Pastor, can you keep this confidential?" Stop them immediately and inform this person that, "If you confess that you are harming a minor through physical or sexual abuse, abusing an elderly person, have committed or intend to commit homicide, are considering suicide or have committed a crime, I will report this information to the proper authorities."

Information relating to a person's medical history has been elevated by HIPAA to a level of confidentiality and is protected by law. As a pastor, I have experienced the negative consequences of what happens when a person enters a hospital and the hospital does not have a clean protocol for chaplain referrals. Clients can be lost and forgotten and their spiritual needs unmet. Educate your church members that when they enter a hospital, especially through the emergency room, the family may have to take the initiative to clear the way for pastoral visits. It is best to contact the hospital chaplain and make a request for your pastor to visit.

Secret 1. Hidden from others; revealed to none or too few; as, keep this matter secret [2]

Secrets and secrecy breed dysfunction. I have heard many times on the playground little children saying to one another, "Keep this a secret." In this exchange, the child is testing the quality of the relationship and measures trust and endurance as building blocks for long-term friendship. In the church arena, secrets have no place. If someone asks you to keep a secret, your first response is, "No! Not unless you can convince me of the benefits to do so." After a short explanation, the information shared, if valuable, usually falls under privileged information or may even be elevated to confidential.

I was on the playground watching the children play when a third-grade girl walked up to me with a sheepish look and said very quietly, "Father Bill, can you keep a secret?"

I leaned down to whisper back to her, "No, I don't like to keep secrets."

The little girl looked at me and said, "But this is very important, and I promised I would not tell anyone about it."

I replied, "Well maybe I can help you. Does the person who asked you to keep this secret need help, or are they in trouble and you don't now how to help them?"

She smiled and said, "Yep, she's in big trouble and I don't know how to help her. She is my best friend and I will keep her secret."

I replied, "Well, if I can help her you will have to let me know what I can do."

The little girl put her finger to her mouth and with her eyes shut she said, "Well, if you heard me speaking to myself about what's wrong, then I could not stop you from helping her."

I replied, "Sounds like a plan."

"Well," said the little girl, "Jenny is stuck under the fence, that we are not supposed to be near, and she can't get out because she will tear her uniform, and she doesn't want to ask the playground teacher because that will get her into trouble, so she thought she would just wait until everybody went back to class, and hopefully the teacher would not miss her from recess, and God would send an angel to help rescue Jenny..." And as this little girl paused to take a short breath, I jumped in and said, "That's more than enough information for me to

we are only as sick as our secrets

go and help Jenny. I will let her know that I heard an angel whisper in my ear that Jenny needed a little help."

I walked toward the school fence and there was Jenny stuck halfway between the playground and the outside sidewalk. With a little twisting and turning and just a small tear of her uniform, Jenny was freed from her captivity. I did make an agreement that she report to her teacher and mother how her uniform got torn and that she had broken a playground rule and that she should own up to the consequences.

Jenny, with a bowed head, commented as she was walking back to the school building, "Nobody told me that angels would help bail you out and then turn you in."

From the mouths of babes, I thought.

There are situations in which a pastoral minister may choose to withhold information from other staff or parish members. Limiting the sharing of information may constitute "keeping some information secret" or "retaining information due to its volatility or negative consequences." Each time a pastoral minister keeps someone's shared information in confidence, it would be good to ask yourself whether the sharing of this information would be a cause for potential harm. Is it necessary to share this information so as to reduce the possibility of gossip and misrepresentation? Would it benefit the overall cause to share this information with others? Is it my privilege to share this information with others?

Internal forum and *external forum* are used in seminaries. "In taking decisions concerning the admission of the candidates to the orders or their admission into the seminary, one can never ask the opinion of the spiritual director and of the confessors."[3] All that is shared with a spiritual director and confessor is protected by internal forum.

Recently, internal forum has been used with lay spiritual directors, adult formation directors and catechists helping converts while participating in the RCIA (Rite of Christian Initiation for Adults). This is a questionable practice because both Canon Law and the Program for Priestly Formation assume that only male-ordained clergy working within the context of a seminary can claim the use of internal forum. I would suggest that information shared between a director and directee be considered confidential information unless matters discussed violate civil law and include mandatory reporting, such as sexual abuse of a minor or the elderly, suicide, and homicide or criminal behavior.

When we speak of internal forum, we refer to conversations that take place under the guarantee of confidentiality. Both spiritual direction and sacramental confession partake of the internal forum. It is a part of the seal of confession that a priest cannot initiate any conversation outside the sacrament of penance with a penitent (or anyone else) about anything mentioned during a confession.[4]

Internal forum has its place with spiritual directors who provide a safe and nonjudgmental environment for a directee to explore his or her life in relation to God. In the seminary, any information shared between seminarian and spiritual director lies within the internal forum. This means that nothing of what is shared can be passed on to any formator, formation committee or rector, pastor, vocation director or bishop.

Disclosure that a seminarian makes in the course of spiritual direction belongs to the internal forum. Consequently, the spiritual director is held to the strictest confidentiality concerning information received in spiritual direction. He may neither reveal it nor use it. The only possible exception to this standard of confidentiality would be the case of grave, immediate or mortal danger involving the directee or another person. If what is revealed in spiritual direction coincides with the celebration of the sacrament of penance (in other words, what is revealed is revealed *ad ordinem absolutionis*), that is, the exchange not only takes place in the internal forum but also the sacramental forum, then the absolute strictures of the seal of confession hold, and no information may be revealed or used.[5]

The external forum allows information shared between two people to be discussed with those who could contribute to a person's formation process, health-care program or through an open referral whereby a client's medical, psychological and family history is discussed with those who can contribute to the client's well-being.

If a pastor is given information from a staff member or church volunteer and this information has legal, moral, ethical or medical consequences, it should be declared that the reporting person will not be mentioned, but action must be taken on behalf of the information given. The federal law called "the Whistle-Blower Act" legally protects people reporting unlawful acts to their place of employment or other authority that could instigate legal action and begin an investigation.

If an employee speaks ill about another employee and makes an accusation, the pastor or acting supervisor needs to follow the written guidelines provided by the diocese for mediation and employee conflict resolution. If by chance you do not have guidelines for intervening and investigating an accusation, here are some that maybe helpful:

- If you can bring in a professional who is trained in mediation, do yourself the favor and contract someone to help you facilitate this conflict.
- If you are without a professional mediator, then including a third person (someone who is a counselor or professional manager and who is not on staff or related to either party) is a must.
- If you are a male pastor and the conflict involves a woman, make sure that you have a female assist in the initial interview.
- If you are a female pastor and the conflict involves a man, make sure that you have a male assist in the initial interview.

The goals of mediation include:

- To gain an increased understanding of the other person
- To exhibit receptivity and a willingness to acknowledge how each person may have contributed to the conflict
- To learn from any mistakes made without retribution or revenge
- To achieve measurable goals for both parties that will enhance their working relationship
- To achieve some level of forgiveness and reconciliation

Before any formal action is taken with the interviews, the accused and the accuser should receive a written outline that explains the process that you hope to implement. It is your hope that both parties will experience justice and mercy. From the first announcement and explanation, both parties must sign an agreement that they will keep the mediation sessions in confidence and that they will not share any information with coworkers, spouses, family, friends, volunteers or any other person. If this is a painful experience for either party, they can be reassured that recourse to a counselor or professional therapist does not violate the confidentiality agreement. If either person needs to take a break during the interview process to prayerfully consider their memory of the situation or to recollect, this can be agreed upon any time during the mediation process.

Steps in the Mediation Process

1. Interview both parties separately with a third person who should help document what is said during the interviews. The interview is an opportunity to help both the accused and accuser to outline their perceptions and beliefs of what they think, feel and want.

2. Include in the interview process two repeated questions: What is your perception of what happened? How would you like this to be resolved?

3. It is helpful to avoid taking sides, asking for either person to speculate why this happened and accepting second- and third-hand information that sounds like gossip and/or slander. Avoid the stockpiling maneuver whereby one of the parties begins to name others who supports and agrees what he or she believes and feels. It may, however, be helpful to document these names and their relation to the conflict with the possibility of including them in the interview process.

4. After both parties (and others involved in the conflict) have been interviewed, a joint meeting of both the accused and the accuser with yourself and a third person as the witness should be held.

5. It can be helpful to write a summary statement of mentioned issues and the proposed resolutions. Begin with an emphasis on resolution and understanding, and try to avoid blaming, judging or accusations that alienate and isolate.

6. For the conjoint session with both the accused and the accuser, negotiate a designated time and place that provide an environment removed from any of the other staff or volunteers who may hear what could be said in case there are loud voices.

7. Both the accused and the accuser should be allowed to speak about their issues after they have read the summary report given by you with the aid of your third-party person.

8. Mediation between the two parties should ensue with an emphasis on an exchange of information to increase both empathy and understanding. Again, repeat the two questions: What is your perception of what happened? How would you like this to be resolved?

9. If there are threats of a lawsuit, or either the accused or accuser demands further action be taken, the pastor should end the session with a referral to a professional mediator, or otherwise the matter should be sent to the proper diocesan office for further action and consultation.

10. If either party walks out of the mediation session, it is best not to pursue the person. Rather, let them cool off and make a phone call the next day and ask if they would like to return to the mediation session. If the person rejects the offer to continue mediation, then a summary report of what happened up to the point of departure can be documented and sent to both parties.

Additional Resources

Consult the bibliography for complete publishing information on the following titles:

Brown, Richard C. *When Ministry Is Messy.*
Carnegie, Dale, and Associates. *Managing Through People.*
Ciarrocchi, Joseph W. *A Minister's Handbook of Mental Disorders.*
Harvey, Eric, and Al Lucia. *144 Ways to Walk the Talk.*
Harvey, Eric, and Steve Ventura. *Walk Awhile in My Shoes.*
Harvey, Eric, and the Walk the Talk Team. *180 Ways to Walk the Customer Service Talk.*
McKenna, Kevin E. *A Concise Guide to Your Rights in the Catholic Church.*
National Press Publications. *The Supervisor's Handbook.*
Nielsen, Duke. *Partnering with Employees.*
Nierenberg, Gerard I. *The Art of Negotiating.*
Thomas, Marlin. *Resolving Disputes in Christian Groups.*

Chapter 6
The Power Shadow in the Helping Professions

Most professions serve the health and well-being of humanity in one way or another. However, the activities of the doctor, priest, teacher, psychotherapist and social worker involve very specialized and deliberate attempts to help the unfortunate, the ill, those who have somehow lost their way. In the following chapters, I will attempt to describe how and why the members of these "ministering professions" can also do the greatest damage—harm caused directly by their very desire to help.[1]

If you have a title, you have power.

The more admired and adored your title, the more power you must manage.

Add the dimension of the spiritual and your power stands close to the divine. Your very position holds you in esteem and the desire to emulate you and follow your every instruction can become all-consuming for the admirer.

As good stewards, those in the helping professions must consciously maintain a belief that as helpers we are nothing more than good stewards of what has been loaned to us. We own nothing. All is gift from God. The real danger begins when helpers convince themselves that they are "the source of power" and they own what has been freely given to them by title and position. Now the power shadow takes hold of the ego and dangerous patterns emerge, like the false prophet, the charlatan and the hypocrite.

Those in the helping professions, clergy especially, are perceived as educated, intelligent, spiritual and understanding in the ways of the divine. The spiritual world infiltrates all aspects of life and has privilege to influence and impact the physical, emotional, intellectual, social, moral, ethical, historical—all of one's choices. To be near someone who is considered privileged, trained, ordained and consecrated amplifies both image and imagination. Illusions of what a relationship with someone like this could be can fictionalize the hopes and dreams of a better quality of life, quick salvation and effortless spiritual growth.

Most people in the helping professions will maintain their contributions to the care and health of those they serve. Honoring the free will of another is a guiding moral imperative. Assisting those we serve with options and resources so that each person can develop their choice-making skills is a measurement of our effectiveness in helping. That is why a professional helper learns early on that giving advice is noneffective and may keep the very person they are helping in a dependent state. Such advice giving encourages codependency, love addiction and enmeshment.

The power shadow consumes common sense and restricts the helper's ability to "let go and let God." The helper, seduced by the power shadow, proclaims, "I know what's best for you; do as I say or else!" The power shadow consumes the freedom of others. The power shadow becomes indignant, "…even when our help is rejected by those concerned. In our own way we frequently force a certain view of life upon others whether they agree to it or not. We do not choose to acknowledge a right to sickness, neurosis, unhealthy familial relations, social degeneracy and eccentricity."[2]

An Example of the Power Shadow

Pastor Rachel has been very successful in her leadership and pastoral guidance during the tumultuous times in her church. She was hired just after the church membership experienced a severe and violent split in the congregation. Half of the members sided with the previous pastor and left with him. The other half decided to stay and rebuild their church membership with the guidance and leadership of a new pastor. Pastor Rachel came with numerous life experiences that were much needed to help reshape and refound this wounded church community. Over the next six months, Pastor Rachel was flawless in her decisions, leadership skills and pastoral direction. The whole church began to sing her praises. There seemed to be no end to her competencies and accomplishments. A few of the church members wanted to begin to reach out to those members who left and invite them back to their church. The word got out that those who left with the previous pastor had became unhappy with his leadership style and direction.

The small contingency of church members approached their new pastor. The church council who advises the pastor was divided over this new idea. Pastor Rachel was not in agreement with inviting those who had left the church, creating so much pain and suffering. Those wanting to begin to reach out with forgiveness and reconciliation were taken back by how adamant Pastor Rachel was toward the idea. Arguments broke out and Pastor Rachel declared, "I am the pastoral and spiritual leader of the church, and obedience to my directions is expected from all the members." After some of the people were able to catch their breath, both those for and against the new idea of reaching out to members who had left became uncomfortable and some were frightened by the power and tone of Pastor Rachel.

The meeting ended with little discussion. Pastor Rachel left fuming. She reports later in a supervisory session, "After all I have done to sacrifice for those people. Now they will not listen to my common sense. How can they undermine my authority? I am the one who brought some order and direction to their mess." I reassured her that, the greater the influence of the (power shadow), the more the helper seems to cling to one's alleged "objectivity." In such cases the discussion of the actions to be taken become blatantly dogmatic, as if there could be only one correct solution to the problem.[3]

After we explored her anger toward those who were perceived as undermining and disobedient, Pastor Rachel began to realize that she was unfamiliar with anyone questioning her decisions, challenging her ideas or criticizing her choices for the church members. Basically, she had become flawless—divine in the eyes of her adorers. Pastor Rachel began to believe in her infallible abilities. The power shadow duped her and blinded her to her own core faith and beliefs: forgiveness, mercy, compassion and ministry to those who had been hurt because of the breakdown within the church membership.

With enough contrition and humility, Pastor Rachel was able to admit she had become drunk on power and authority. Her conviction of group discernment and listening together to the Holy Spirit for guidance had been the cornerstone of her success. With some introspection and supervision Pastor Rachel was able to admit that she overstepped her role as facilitator and healer. It was time for her to replace her opinions with shared ideas and invite those with more compassion than she had displayed to help this church achieve the kind of balance and kindness she had been promoting since her arrival. Pastor Rachel began to embrace the call to become a servant minister to her people. The discovery for Pastor Rachel was to redesign her role as facilitator and move toward empowerment of others through mercy and compassion.

Considering the Power Shadow

The power shadow can consume ego consciousness. It is created when a person with title, position, authority and influence denies their need to be flawless, to dominate, control and manipulate others. The more a person is controlled by the power shadow the more they will make questionable decisions, exempt themselves from morals and ethics, put themselves above and outside the law, excuse themselves from responsibility for the harmful and negative consequences they cause others, minimize the care of others and interpret the suffering of others as a necessary cost to be paid for mistakes made.

A cleric or pastoral leader who has been duped by the power shadow may take on the behaviors of "someone who interferes whenever possible, forcing his will on people without really understanding what is going on, trying to bring everything into line according to narrow, moralistic, bourgeois standards, prompted by a delight in power, insulted and malicious when his power is not acknowledged."[4] Remember that the struggle with the power shadow rarely impacts the cynical and indifferent individual who simply does their job formally and correctly. This does not reduce their creativity to either positive or negative; rather, it keeps them in the middle of bland, boring and monotonous.

The power shadow affects the pastor and parish leader who is emotionally engaged and charged with excitement. This is the parish leader who is enthusiastic, on fire and dedicated. This is the parish volunteer who has devoted hours of his/her time, talent and treasure who will have to bring to consciousness the sweet taste of power and compensate consciously with deference, humility, empathy, inclusion, tenderness, taking turns and listening. As soon as the helper can admit limitation, weakness, receive intimacy from others, become vulnerable and share both pain and grief through storytelling and self-disclosure can he or she take control of the toxic consequences of the power shadow.

The False Prophet

The shadow of the false prophet is the dark sibling to all pastors, parish leaders and volunteers. Here the false prophet asks others to accomplish what that individual has never attained. The false prophet demands from others what is unfamiliar to himself.

"Don't do as I do; do as I say!" becomes the pulpit proclamation of the false prophet. This shadow will portray the clergy and parish leader as better than he or she really is.

The pastor consumed by the false prophet will preach with moral certitude and lay heavy burdens on their church members. Guilt, shame and irrational expectations are heaped upon the heads of those who see the preacher and teacher as omniscient—standing close to the source of all that is holy and good. The adorers of the false prophet hang on their every word, believing him or her to be divinely inspired.

The knowledge of God plays a central role in the ideal model of pastor and parish leader. Those who become fanatical about their own intentions and maintain an absolute certainty of their own interpretations welcome their dark sibling who will concretize the irrational and help convince others, "Either join me and be amongst the righteous or leave me and become one of the damned." Clergy and parish leaders who embrace the false prophet create a world that is black and white. There is no room for gray. Obsessive and compulsive behaviors are demanded from all who want to affiliate with the false prophet. Spiritual and physical health, sanity and demonic possession and personal and family well-being are defined with stringent, punitive and fanatical dictates given by the false prophet. One's template is limited and constricted and usually leaves the majority of people wanting and excluded.

The false prophet is but one dimension of the power shadow.

An Example of the False Prophet

Father Ben has been ordained for two years. He has prided himself on being a conservative Roman Catholic and believes that true Catholicism lies in what used to be and not what we have today. Father

Ben comes from a rural diocese and is assigned as a pastor to a vibrant, contemporary post–Vatican II church.

In this church they have been promoting stewardship of time, talent and treasure. Of the thousand registered families, St. Agatha has become a role-model church in its success in promoting volunteerism with over one hundred committees providing a wide range of services and ministries. The parish also prides itself on its youth ministry, which has developed four youth music choirs, each writing, publishing and providing music at four of the weekend masses.

Having been to this parish, I was in awe at the joy, friendliness and hospitality I experienced while attending a weekend mass. In less than six months, Father Ben as the new pastor had discerned that St. Agatha was not a "true Roman Catholic Church" and that it was time this parish church returned to its origins. He shut down all four youth music groups and had the present hymnals replaced with a traditional music publication. He hired an organist who was given the preapproved music list most of which was either Latin or required a cantor. The many service committees were slowly suspended because Father Ben found that it was too much for him to attend and supervise all of those committees. Within the year, the family enrollment dropped from one thousand families down to six hundred families. The offertory was reduced by 40 percent. The bishop sent in a team to study what was going on to cause the reduction in offertory and attendance. The final report outlined how Father Ben was unable to appreciate what was working well at St. Agatha and that his pastoral leadership style could not acclimate to this contemporary stewardship church. In addition, the report mentioned that Father Ben's leadership style would be better appreciated in a small church with an older congregation who would enjoy a more sovereign leadership style.

The false prophet can rule the pastor or parish leader who may actually have some capacity for empathy, effective listening, spiritual guidance, spiritual direction, Christian counseling and healing of memories or laying on of hands for physical healing. The false prophet can create a following of people who become dazed in their belief that they can vicariously feel elevated by God and special to God through a fellowship with the pastor or parish leader.

C. J. Jung repeatedly pointed out that whenever a bright psychic content becomes lodged in consciousness (e.g., "I can help people out of their pain," or "I can help you understand where God is in all this mess, or "My training allows me to be effective in helping you"), its opposite is constellated in the unconscious and tries to do harm from that vantage point ("If you do what I tell you, you are guaranteed relief," or "I know what God is trying to tell you," or "I know more than you; that is why you should listen to me"). The physician becomes a charlatan precisely because he wants to heal as many people as possible; the clergyman becomes a hypocrite and false prophet precisely because he wants to bring people to the true faith; and the psychotherapist becomes an unconscious charlatan and false prophet although he works day and night on becoming more conscious.[5]

Every charlatan has to wield a double-edged sword. Along with managing the desire to be great and influential comes the additional challenge of dealing with the longing and desire of those they serve who want them to be mighty, effective and powerful. Many of our parishioners, church members and clients want us to have the "magic wand." With a quick flip of the wrist, some expect us to relieve them of their pain with little or no effort and discomfort and all in one session.

Emphasizing the few who may have a quick resolution to their problems, the charlatan builds on this perception and can deceive others into thinking that everybody will have the same results if only they "believed enough" in God or the charlatan. For those who do not get the relief, it is their fault for having a lack of faith. For those who do find relief, look how powerful and wonderful the charlatan can be. The charlatan urges the needy person to avoid the long, difficult path to a genuine cure. In this case the charlatan's concern is not for the true healing of the patient but for his own image as a great healer.[6]

I was attending a healing mass for those who had lost family members due to suicide, homicide, abortion, perinatal loss, divorce or tragic death. The priest who was the main celebrant of the mass gave a homily in which he declared that by completing a simple prayer he wrote—every person in your family system—those living and deceased—would be completely healed. He was holding these prayer cards in one hand while in the other hand he suggested you make a financial contribution to his ministry. I was appalled and astonished at how many people ran roughshod over those in front of them and pushed their way to the front to lay hold of the "magic prayer card" that would set their entire family free of all pain and grief.

For those who were desperate or vulnerable enough, I couldn't help but feel anger for how this charlatan took hold of their heart-strings and pulled hard to get them to believe in his quick fix. For those who did hesitate, the priest quickly reprimanded us and informed us that our lack of faith kept our families in bondage and that our unwillingness to believe was a serious mistake on our part.

After the service was over, I went directly to him and asked how he could help relieve my pain. I told him that my pain came from the false promise he made to all these wounded souls; that one simple prayer and one mass could determine the free will of each person prayed for. He gasped and declared, "Even God would not compromise our free will."

I spoke loud enough to be heard by anyone standing around me, "You just promised that if I say this prayer, I could determine the free will of each of my family members."

He declared, "That's not what I meant."

I preceded to speak even louder, "It is what you promised with your prayer." He turned and walked away.

I believe that prayer can open doors for people to lift their feet and walk through. I believe in what Pope John Paul II said, "Conversion, penance and prayer can change the course of history."[7] I believe that prayer can open the heart and mind of a person and God's grace can pour through and activate the change process. I believe that "Grace builds on nature." Through the power of intercessory prayer God can do for you what you cannot do for yourself. I also believe that where there is growth there is pain. If you avoid or skip the pain, you do not get the growth. If you embrace the pain, you will discover the growth.

The reassurance we Christians have is that all pain bears a gift. In our theology of redemptive suffering we have been reminded that God's presence can be found in the mess. All pain, whether it is physical, spiritual, social, and emotional or intellectual, has a message to be learned. Pain is not the enemy. Pain is the messenger. "The information it has about our life can be remarkably specific, but it usually falls into one of two categories: "We would be more alive if we did more of this," and, "Life would be more lovely if we did less of that." Once we get the pain's message, and follow its advice, the pain goes away."[8] Victor Frankl states that one of the worst things you can do to the human per-

Pain is not the enemy. Pain is the messenger.

son is pull them from their pain prematurely. In doing so, you have deprived them of a growth experience.

The charlatan does not honor the pain of others. They are more interested in their claim to fame and how much attention their work can provoke. The charlatan lives for the appreciation of others like a drug addict waiting for his next fix. Charlatans search out the wounded and needy so that they can exercise their influence and become the wonder worker, the chosen one, the sorcerer and the anointed one.

I met a woman who was referred to me by her pastor. Supposedly this woman was having apparitions of the Blessed Mother. I was to assess her and give some feedback to the pastor on how to handle the growing amount of followers who have declared her "holy" and "hand-picked" by Mary, the Mother of Jesus. Before this visionary came into my office two of her followers walked into the Mercy Center and sprinkled holy water and blessed salt from the front door to the back of the building where my office was located. Then as they approached my door they gave me a good dosing of holy water and sprinkled me with the blessed salts. This was to ensure that evil spirits would not harm the visionary. Needless to say, I was already starting to become irritated.

Her two followers then proceeded to inform me of how it was a privilege for me to have quality time alone with the visionary. I reassured them that it was time for them to leave my office and if they were to shake any more salt onto the carpet I would demand that they take time to vacuum up their mess.

In comes the visionary. At first sight I could see the bags under her eyes and that her skin looked ashen grey. Her hair was dull and she looked sickly. After introducing myself, I explained that her pastor sent her to me so that I could "discern" and assess what was happening to her and if it was of God. The woman gasped and exclaimed, "Only the Blessed Mother can tell me what is of God." I reassured her that I would do my best to cooperate with God and the Blessed Mother, and asked that she also be obedient to her pastor's wishes and cooperate with my interview.

After a few quick questions I discovered that this visionary's husband left her because of her religious fanaticism and that her three adult children were ashamed of her, especially because she keeps claiming how special she is to the Blessed Mother. After I reviewed her diet and concluded she was suffering from malnutrition, sleep deprivation and bruises from head to toe from self-imposed sadistic penitential practices, the visionary was getting impatient with me. She could not understand why I had not asked her about the beautiful visions she'd had and all the special messages that Our Lady had given to her. I reminded her that the pastor was concerned that her family life was a mess, her self-imposed health care was pitiful and the people following and promoting her were not well people.

As she stood up to leave, she declared, "The Blessed Mother has given me permission to disregard your opinions and inform you that they are not from God."

I responded quickly and said, "Well, I do know that the Blessed Mother regards obedience to church authority as a nonnegotiable, and obedience to church authority is the quickest way to test whether what you are experiencing is from God." She sat down immediately.

I continued with my final point of discernment, "Now, to find out if your visions are from God and are authentic, I would like you to inform the Blessed Mother that she may not appear to you anymore. If she wants to direct a message to you, she will have to speak to me first. If you cooperate, then it is the wisdom of the church that sincere obedience is one step in discernment to confirm that your visions are from God. If not, then you must be creating these visions for your own purposes."

She immediately stood up and, looking down at me, declared that I was not going to tell her what she could or could not do. As she left my office she yelled at me and said, "You sound just like my husband and selfish children. It's always about them."

Within a few months the woman had over one hundred men and women attending her so-called apparitions in her home. The pastor, in consultation with his bishop and me, had to make a public statement about the credibility of this woman and her alleged visions. The woman, after two years, still has a small following of men and women who are convinced that she sees and converses with the Blessed Mother.

Remember that the shadow is the reverse side of your personal, family, cultural and religious beliefs. The shadow contains all those thoughts, feelings, desires and behaviors that your ego has determined unacceptable. The shadow bucket, as I like to call it, needs to be inventoried and emptied frequently so that it does not overflow into your daily activities. When the shadow bucket is not emptied through introspection, dream work, journaling, storytelling, confession, spiritual direction or counseling—the leakage can become very toxic.

Toxic shadow content denies its existence. For example, "I'll never be like my angry mother or alcoholic father or abusive husband or nagging wife." The more you deny its possibility the more you become it. To lay hold of the shadow and empty the bucket takes humility, contrition, honest self-disclosure, a willingness to admit weaknesses and confess to another significant person those qualities you would like to bury and hide.

Shadow work is a moral imperative for those in the helping profession. The potential for shadow implosions grow when we do not take the time to review our own inventory of imperfections. This cannot be done in isolation or alone. For the ego to take ownership of the shadow content, the ego has to be known by a significant other. The ego has to say out loud to another person so that—the ego knows that another knows. Then and only then is there shadow integration. To lie or deny the shadow content is to allow it to grow in strength and propensity. With continual denial of shadow content, the ego can become self-absorbed. So much so, that a person is unable to see, hear and think clearly exactly what they are doing and the impact they're having on the lives of others.

Another dimension of the charlatan's shadow is its capacity for "vicarious living." This means that what a person longs for and desires but cannot have because of family, cultural and religious beliefs can be accessed through the entertainment of another person's life experiences.

Vicarious Living

Sister Karen, a religious sister, has befriended a single man, age thirty-two, who admits he is a sex addict. Sister Karen has become this man's spiritual director. Daniel, the spiritual directee, has admitted to Sister Karen that he has not found any relief in his acting out. He has been to support groups and tried various medications. He does feel loved and accepted by Sister Karen, who always makes time for him. Sister Karen admitted while in supervision that she had become overly attached to Daniel and that she was sometimes meeting with him daily for an update on all his sexual encounters.

In reviewing her spiritual direction skills, it became apparent that this celibate woman was vicariously exploring sexual perversions, sexual acting out and the details of sexual encounters through Daniel's stories. She admitted that her fascination with Daniel's stories would sweep her off her feet and she would blush, sweat, sometimes moan and feel enraptured while he spoke. Her undying attention and open schedule gave Daniel a false sense of inclusion and made him feel special and wanted. Sister Karen realized that she had become the charlatan by vicariously living through the thrills, ecstasy and agony of Daniel's sexual addiction.

Pastor Ed shares that he is seeing a married woman who is having an affair with another man. Pastor Ed is unhappily married and has not pursued any marriage counseling because he believes it would jeopardize his standing as pastor of a large and wealthy church. Pastor Ed finds that he covets his pastoral counseling sessions with Mary, the married woman having an affair. Pastor Ed has found himself enjoying the details of her schemes and the intensity of her sexual encounters. Pastor Ed has also admitted that he finds himself fantasizing about this married woman and at times imagining that he is the man she is having an affair with.

Pastor Ed was advised to refer Mary to a female counselor. It had become obvious that the pastoral counseling of eight sessions had been nonproductive. Pastor Ed is alarmed at the suggestion and cancels his next two appointments for supervision. One month later, Pastor Ed calls in a panic. His wife has filed for a divorce because she had caught Pastor Ed with his client having frequent dinners at an expensive restaurant. I refer Pastor Ed to a marriage counselor while he and I explore the vicarious fantasies he had been sponsoring with his client.

In this sense it is true, as Jung says, that an analyst (pastor) can give only to his patients (church members) that which he has himself.[9]

"In order to break free of the vicious cycle of the charlatan, false prophet and hypocrite, the clergy and parish leader must expose themselves to something which touches them deeply, something unlike their daily routine and which would throw them off balance, stimulate them, show them time and again who they really are, how weak and pompous, how vain and narrow. The depths of the shadow must be plumbed in love."[10]

The shadow entanglement can be penetrated through friendship. Friendship, loving but forceful encounters with one's equals, to attack and be attacked, to insult and be insulted; all of this strikes again and again at the psychic center of those involved. The clergy and parish leaders need symmetrical relationships, relationships with partners who are their equals, friends who dare to confront and challenge, to point out not just virtues but vices, weaknesses, flaws and defects.

The important thing is the involvement, the joy and sorrow, the disappointment and surprise, which flows back and forth between people who love one another.[11] Only through the emotional interchange with those to whom he/she stands in a relation of love can a new dimension be brought into his/her benumbed world.[12]

To crack open the power shadow a person in the helping profession needs direct contact with acts of humility, time with nonproductive fun, intense and authentic human relationships, time for introspection and meditation, review of one's personal inventory that explores the potential for evil, wrongdoing, manipulation and misuse of power. When the opportunity arises for the helper to admit fault, error and wrongdoing, these encounters are like a release valve for the power shadow and depletes the toxic arrogance and false pride of the helper.

Ultimately, the saints and holy men and women who embraced moments of humility confessed and learned from their mistakes, becoming powerful forces of influence in their time. Dr. Marie-Louise von Franz and Barbara Hannah, who shared a household in Kusnacht, Switzerland, had the custom of requiring whoever had some especially good fortune to carry out the garbage for the week.[13] This simple act allowed the successful student to balance their shadow side of something positive. If left unattended, the shadow side of success can become the stumbling stone for others to trip over, if not fall down the cliffs of unconsciousness.

At the Mercy Center, we host men and women religious from around the world. On this particular thirteen-week sabbatical we had a religious sister who had served for eighteen years as her order's international superior. Many of the sisters were underground, living in very dangerous situations, and the international superior had to be skilled at slipping in and out of countries that did not want nuns providing service and ministry to the poor, especially women and young uneducated girls.

Sister Jean Mary had been reelected because she was tough, smart and had the skills to manage an international religious congregation. Over the years she had become "a soldier for Christ," and much of her tenderness, gentleness and playfulness went underground. The new international superior wrote to the Mercy Center and asked if we could help "tenderize" Sister Jean Mary. Those who were now living with her in community found her difficult to be with her because she was so hard-hearted.

Sister Jean Mary had a lot of people who were at her command. The power shadow was at her beck-and-call, and she knew how to flex her muscles when needed. The first day I meet Sister Jean Mary and shook her hand, it felt like shaking the hand of a professional wrestler. I noticed that she did not smile, the creases in her face made her look prematurely aged and she walked like a stiff board.

At the Mercy Center, each person is assigned a housecleaning chore. Sister Jean Mary was given the assignment to clean the two bathrooms at the front entrance of the Mercy Center. She rebelled and declared to the executive director that this menial task was beneath her. She had no idea that the executive director could butt heads with the most stubborn of program participants.

Sister Jean Mary was reminded that her assignment was her responsibility and that the humility required for such a simple task was not beneath her call to holiness. During the next few weeks, the program participants noticed that Sister Jean Mary had become tender and more playful. The more we teased her about cleaning the bathrooms and got her to laugh, the more she smiled and softened up. Her power shadow had been punctured, and now there was room in her ego to expand her potential for relationship, laughter and nonproductive fun.

To be an effective leader, one needs power and control. The effective helper needs to have some useful skill that can be offered to another so as to enhance their quality of life. Each of us who are professional helpers spends years learning our trade and developing our talents. When you begin to add up the workshops, classes and degrees that are required to be a professional helper, each rung in the ladder of success assumes personal and professional power.

Struggles and challenges must be conquered. The joy of success and the agony of failure refine our professional persona. Learning from our mistakes is a value to be cherished. Shame, guilt, debasement and "stinking thinking" are the manure for growing false pride that feeds the power shadow. If you cannot make a mistake and learn from it, then you are condemned to repeat it. Even worse, those who need help and service will suffer from the unconscious power drive of those helpers who maintain and live off the life energy of others for their own pleasure of success.

Now that you understand the importance of owning and bringing to consciousness your power shadow—let's explore what happens when the shadow becomes projected onto others.

Additional Resources

Consult the bibliography for complete publishing information on the following titles:

Aron, Elaine N. *The Highly Sensitive Person*.
Clark, Stephen B. *Building Christian Communities*.
Guggenbuhl-Craig, Adolf. *Power in the Helping Professions*.
Johnson, Robert A. *Owning Your Own Shadow*.
Walk the Talk Resources. *Leading with Values*.

Chapter 7
Pastoral Leaders and Projections
Fatal-Attraction Syndrome, Understanding Infatuations and Repulsions

Over the past twelve years I have worked with numerous seminarians and religious men and women as novices and have given them the three promises of the helping profession as a pastor, parish leader, religious sister or brother, principal, or teacher:

1. You will be falsely accused; know your rights and have good consultors advise you.
2. You will fall in love, if not become infatuated; deal with it with your spiritual director, confessor or counselor.
3. You will experience fatal-attraction syndrome; someone will fall in love with you and unconsciously convince themselves that you love them as much as they unconsciously love you.

With regard to the third point, when you do not return an infatuated person's gestures of affection, the negative affections kick in. As high up as they elevate you with admiration and singular devotion, imagine that is how low they will take you to achieve any sense of balance and proportion. One day you walk on water, the next day you've inundated them. One day you can turn water into wine and the next day you make sour vinegar. One day the fatally attracted sing your praises and the next day they speak about how bad you are.

Fatal-attraction syndrome happens when a person has a fractured ego and you become their missing piece. The relationship may have begun innocently enough, for example, spending time together working on a project with other people involved. Then this volunteer may begin to imagine that you are more delighted with their contributions and begin to feel special in your presence. A few notes are left in your parish mailbox with an emphasis on how wonderful you are to work with. After a while, this wounded soul begins to intensify their connections with you by spending more time at every parish function. The person comes early and is the last to leave. The notes of appreciation now begin to take on letters of deep affection and longing to be with you outside of parish ministry time.

The turning point that propels the fatal-attraction syndrome to become volatile occurs when the person being admired does not catch on to these subtle gestures of befriending and does not return the sender's unconscious love and affection. The attraction becomes fractured and the flaws of the one most loved and admired now become amplified. The depth of love becomes the height of disgust and repulsion. The priest, pastor, religious sister or brother, the youth minister, or director of music now becomes the target of anger, rage, hatred and revenge. As the target, you may have no idea why this person picked you out of the crowd of leaders. Here are some simple rules to keep in mind while you manage a fatal-attraction experience:

1. You may never know why you were chosen to be a point of projection and ended up involved in a fatal-attraction experience.
2. Never keep a fatal attraction a secret. Tell those you work with and report it immediately to your supervisor, dean, bishop or advisory council.
3. Ask someone who is one step higher than your authority to assist you with a direct intervention with the person who is caught up in the fatal-attraction syndrome. This helps divide the negative projection and will reduce some of the fallout that will happen as the fatally attracted person begins to rebound from intense love and affection to anger, revenge and retribution.

Examples of Fatal-Attraction Syndrome

Sarah the Youth Minister

Sarah is a youth minister in a growing congregation. She got her degree in youth formation and ministry development from an esteemed university. Sarah was hired as part of a five-person team to reach out to children and youth from elementary school to college-level students and single adults. Sarah was assigned to work with the college-level students. She was an attractive single female who could sing, play the guitar, dance, teach with enthusiasm, pray with energy and engage the other students to be the best they could be. John, a single male college student joined a sharing group that Sarah had formed. There were about fifteen to twenty other college students who met twice a week for a shared meal, prayer and faith sharing. John was shy, but in time really became freed up to share and laugh with his fellow students. Sarah was good at teasing and bantering with each of the students and does not recall ever giving more attention to John than the other students.

John had asked Sarah to have dinner with him outside of the regular Tuesday and Thursday meals. Sarah thanked John and reassured him that it would not be appropriate for her to engage in a social relationship with him. During the next few weeks John had become withdrawn while attending the twice-a-week dinner and shared prayer and faith. Sarah asked John during one of the breaks if he was feeling all right. John spoke with intense anger that it was none of her business how he felt. Sarah was taken aback and left John to engage some of the other students who did acknowledge how surprised they were at John's tone, volume and posture. The other students perceived John as raging toward Sarah.

Sarah brought this incident to the team and during their process someone mentioned the idea of infatuation and the possibility of a fatal-attraction syndrome. Sarah reflected that she had no memory of ever encouraging John's affections in any special way. She thought that maybe she had done or said something that might have sparked this attraction. Sarah was reassured that some attractions are a one-way street and that she probably didn't do anything but be herself, which would have been enough for John to project his unrealistic feelings and expectations onto Sarah.

A week later Sarah had received numerous phone calls with no message; just hard breathing and a cynical laughter before the person hung up. It was evident to Sarah and the senior youth pastor that it was a man's voice. Suspicions that it was John became more alarming when Sarah began to receive letters taped to her front door, her car windshield and then her office door. These letters were mean, incriminating and vulgar in their criticisms toward Sarah. She was heartbroken and began to feel unsafe while driving to her apartment, where she lived alone.

Sarah's senior pastor called me at the Mercy Center, and we discussed the progression of Sarah's stalker. When someone leaves unsigned messages and letters and begins to threaten or intimidate, this is evidence that someone has begun criminal behavior. When frequent phone calls are made to a person's private home and they become a nuisance and intimidate a person, this is evidence of criminal behavior.

The senior pastor and I met with Sarah and the other youth ministers and designed intervention plans. At the next college youth evening meal, I was asked to meet with the students and explain what was happening to Sarah. The entire youth ministry staff was present, including Sarah. That night, to our good fortune, John was at the meeting. There were over twenty young college students present.

I explained that Sarah has been threatened and intimidated by a male person who has been leaving letters and making anonymous phone calls. I further explained that this intimidating behavior was inappropriate and illegal. ("When the impulses and desires of one person are allowed to supersede the legal and moral rights of others...abuse occurs."[1])

It was the decision of the senior pastor and the church pastor to prosecute whoever was stalking Sarah. A lawyer was contracted and the investigation began. Anyone with information was asked to come forward and speak to Father Bill or the lawyer. If by chance anyone knew who was doing this to Sarah, they could contact Father Bill. He would offer a confidential counseling session for this person who was stalking Sarah. The purpose of the counseling session is to help this person explore his/her need to threaten and intimidate another person and move toward recovery and reconciliation.

A handout, *A Safe Home* (Parent's Place, 1992), was given and discussed in small groups.

<blockquote>

This Home is a Human Sanctuary

In This House—

We give nonviolent consequences.

We encourage each other.

Each person is an individual.

Everyone is responsible for his/her own mess and success.

Everyone is allowed to feel good about his/her own body, and have a safe "bubble" of space.

We talk openly about feelings and problems.

We don't hit or hurt anyone.

We don't put each other down or call each other names.

No one is unfavorably compared to someone else.

No one is rescued from learning the important lessons of life (unless they are in danger of harming themselves or others).

No one is tricked, forced, or trapped into unwanted sexual touching.

Big problems are never a secret to be "swept" under the rug.
</blockquote>

The meeting ended with prayer and faith sharing. John never returned to the biweekly college youth gathering. Sarah stopped receiving the phone calls and the letters. Four months later, we were informed that John had committed suicide in his college dorm room. His roommates shared with the youth ministry team that John had become dependent on alcohol and drugs and would no longer spend time with his few friends. His parents were devastated and at the biweekly dinners, the college students spent weeks exploring their feelings and emotions about John's suicide and the terrible loss of a human person because of alcohol and drugs.

Father Joe the Country Pastor

Father Joe is pastor of a small rural church. He is a vibrant homilist, young, handsome and charismatic. His small congregation loves his energy, and he is a hard worker, developing new services and ministries for this little church community. Mrs. Jenkins has been a widow for about twenty years and has always been a significant contributor both in time and treasure to this church. Father Joe relies on Mrs. Jenkins to learn about the particular needs of this country parish and discovers that it is easy to spend time with Mrs. Jenkins as she fills his mind with stories of how this community survived tornadoes, draughts and wildfires.

During the first year of ministry, Father Joe enjoyed afternoon tea with Mrs. Jenkins. When he did not show for tea, Mrs. Jenkins would call Father Joe and leave messages that bordered on orders and reprimands. Father Joe's popularity grew, and other parishioners wanted him to spend time with them, inviting him for meals and weekend activities. Mrs. Jenkins began to feel left out because other parishioners were taking away her special time with Father Joe.

The day of reckoning between Father Joe and Mrs. Jenkins took place one day when Father Joe forgot to call and inform Mrs. Jenkins that he would not make it to her home for afternoon tea. Father Joe was deeply involved helping a family prepare a funeral for their teenaged son who had died in an automobile accident. Mrs. Jenkins met Father Joe at the rectory on the front porch and began her scolding. She started by listing all his faults and defects and how ungrateful he was for all that she had done for "his" parish community. She felt used by Father Joe and did not want to ever see him again. Mrs. Jenkins declared that she would not be contributing a dime to "Father Joe or his parish."

Father Joe tried to speak to Mrs. Jenkins, to explain that he had forgotten to call her because of the funeral. He paused and realized that something was terribly wrong with Mrs. Jenkins's expectations of him as a person and as a pastor. Mrs. Jenkins departed quickly while still ranting and raving about what a terrible person Father Joe had become. Father Joe wrote Mrs. Jenkins a letter to inform her that he was sorry for the oversight of not canceling his time with Mrs. Jenkins. He also mentioned that as he has come to know more of the church members, he felt it important as pastor that he spend more of his time with all them. It was not his intention to form an exclusive relationship with Mrs. Jenkins at the expense of not doing his job effectively as the pastor. If Mrs. Jenkins wanted to spend some time with him and have afternoon tea, Father Joe would welcome the opportunity. Father Joe never heard from Mrs. Jenkins, and she never attended church again until he left six years later and the new pastor came to town. The first person at the rectory to greet the new pastor was Mrs. Jenkins, who invited the pastor for afternoon tea.

Dealing with Projections

Unless we do conscious work on it, the shadow is almost always projected: that is, it is neatly laid on someone or something else so we do not have to take responsibility for it.[2]

Infatuations and repulsions can provide raw material for personal and professional growth. When a parish leader openly "wears" the qualities and characteristics that are undeveloped in another person, he or she can become a walking target for projections. Every pastoral leader, bishop, priest, pastor, religious sister or brother becomes the loving and hateful mother and father of everyone they serve. Learning how to navigate the waters of projections can either provide an exhilarating ride on the whitecaps of ministry or a terrifying encounter with ocean storms.

When a church member comes up to you and begins to rave about how wonderful you are and that you are the best thing since sliced bread; when this church member wants to hug and kiss you because you are the answer to their prayers; when the member proclaims that every word that comes from you is truly the word of God; and when this church member has only known you for about a week—Beware! Infatuation is at hand.

The quick love and affection given to those in pastoral ministry without the paid dues of time, effort, sacrifice and suffering will put the pastoral leader under a glass bowl so that they can be preserved and protected as well as suffocated. Faults and weaknesses are diminished or viewed as nonexistent. Everything about the pastoral minister that screams of perfection may lead to him or her being perceived as one who lives on the edge of divinity. When this much unearned and unwarranted admiration comes your way, immediately bring out your invisible pin and pop the infatuation bubble that your admirer suffers from. Otherwise be prepared for the roller coaster ride of your life. As high up in admiration and affection he/she feels toward you is the measurement for how low he/she must take you in criticism and berating to achieve a small amount of balance and consciousness.

When infatuation takes hold of one of your admirers, become aware of their unrealistic expectations, such as:

- You should know everything.
- You can do everything without struggle.
- You don't make mistakes.
- I only feel this way when I am with you.
- No one else has been able to help me as much as you have.
- What do you mean you are tired and need a break—I thought you had endless energy and power?
- How could your feelings be hurt? You are above feelings and emotions.
- How could you not be available when I need you?
- You actually need help from others?

Church ministers have a pastoral obligation to help detoxify the intoxication of infatuation of those we serve. In my twenty-eight years of ministry, I have collected some wonderful stories of men and women in pastoral leadership who have been merciful in their outreach to church members who fell head over heels into infatuation.

Examples of Mercy in Action

Margaret the Spiritual Director

Margaret was providing spiritual direction for a widowed husband with three children all under the age of seven. The husband, Joe, could not grieve and admitted that he had not shed a single tear since his wife died quickly of breast cancer. Margaret noticed in her second session with Joe that she was experiencing a strong movement of grief and began to release her tears as Joe was describing how much he loved and missed his wife. Joe noticed the tears and he himself began to cry. After an hour of shared tears, the spiritual direction session ended and Joe was demonstrative in showing his affection to Margaret, and hugged and held her a little longer then Margaret was comfortable with. Margaret mentioned this experience while in supervision, and she was reminded that Joe had a tremendous release with her help. Margaret was able to help Joe into that vulnerable and intimate place called grief. In the group supervision, Margaret was encouraged to communicate her desire to see Joe evolve in his grief but that any further demonstrations of prolonged affection seemed out of place.

The next session of spiritual direction with Joe again entailed prolonged periods of crying. Joe expressed that he had never shared a moment of crying with anyone but his wife. When the session had ended, Margaret forgot to communicate to Joe beforehand that she would prefer that they not hug, but rather shake hands for the departing ritual. Joe hugged Margaret and this time kissed her on the neck. Margaret was very uncomfortable with this gesture and asked Joe if he would wait a few minutes before leaving.

Margaret came into the staff room, and there were two other female staff that had been part of the group supervision. Margaret was flustered and explained how the session went and that she forgot to share with Joe the limits she would like to establish in how they exchanged a departing gesture of affection. Each of the staff reassured Margaret that she needed to inform Joe that she appreciated his trust and honored the vulnerability he shared with her. The gesture of hugging and now kissing on the neck were not appropriate gestures to be shared between the two of them. With some reassurance Margaret went back into her office and shared with Joe her concerns.

At first Joe was hurt and taken back. He tried to rationalize what he was sharing with Margaret, and then something calming came over him. He mentioned that when he hugged his wife, it was agreed between the two of them that he determine how long the hug went on because she always wanted him to hold her longer. He then admitted that the kiss on the neck was something he also added to the affection he shared with his wife before he left for work. Joe smiled and the tears came. Margaret reassured him that his rituals of affection were dear and special between Joe and his wife. Margaret also reassured Joe that his need to hold and be held by a woman was normal but that she could not provide for that particular need. Margaret went on to say that Joe was doing well in his spiritual direction and that if he could manage to work within the limits Margaret was setting between them, they could continue to work together.

Joe smiled, and when he stood up he put out his hand for a handshake and said, "Thanks for your honesty. Thanks for not letting my needs chase you away. My trust in you has just multiplied. I know I can come to you and wear my insides on the outside and you will handle me with tough love. Thank you."

Jonathan the College Student

Jonathan was nineteen years old and naive for someone his age. He had not dated anyone during high school. As a first-year college student, he was realizing that girls found him to be attractive and teased him during some of their shared classes. Jonathan befriended Barbara, the lay campus minister, who was dynamic and charismatic. The young college students were drawn to Barbara. Barbara picked up quickly that Jonathan was flirting with her and that his gestures of affection were getting beyond the acceptable limits of a friendly chaplain-student relationship. Some of the other college students even joked with Jonathan about his "puppy love" with Barbara.

Barbara invited Jonathan to her office and explained that she was picking up gestures of affection and flirting from Jonathan, and wanted to clarify her relationship with him. Jonathan had enough insight to admit that he found Barbara very attractive and that he felt alive when he was around her. Barbara validated Jonathan's feelings and invited him to broaden his capacity to feel and relate to others in the group and not put all his eggs in one basket. Barbara clarified that her role was to be a companion to all the college students and not be particular or exclusive with any one of them. She went on to say that she appreciated Jonathan's warmth and kindness, and that she hoped that he would share in more of the college programs, where he could be loved and befriended by so many other women and men. Barbara noticed that Jonathan was blushing, and she wished him the best in his growth and said she'd look forward to his future participation in the college youth program.

A couple of months passed by, and Jonathan did not attend any of the college programs. Barbara thought it best not to pursue Jonathan. Just before spring break, Barbara's office provided a weekend retreat, and to her surprise Jonathan attended. He was bashful in the beginning and would not make eye contact with Barbara. By Saturday night, Jonathan was more engaging, and by Sunday, shared with his small group that he had an "awakening moment" that helped him grow up. He thanked those who were part of the college campus staff and the other college students for being patient with his immaturity. He looked at Barbara and said, "There are some really kind people who work in campus ministry that are willing to help you grow up and become a healthy adult; you just have to look and listen for the learning moments. I am glad that I did."

Jonathan continued with his participation in many of the campus ministry programs, and by the end of his senior year had fallen deeply in love with Jennifer, another college student. They both attended the spring retreat and shared how they have both grown and how grateful they are that the staff of the campus ministry had been honest and helpful in their growth as young Christian adults. Jonathan even made a joke about his "puppy love experience" his first year in college. No names were mentioned, but Barbara knew who his secret love was.

Repulsions

Repulsions are the dark side of projections. I read in a management-training book that 99 percent of personnel conflict stems from unresolved projections. Repulsions occur when something within our self is unloved and someone has the audacity to wear it out loud. That which we dislike the most about our self becomes the mud we throw at others with repulsion. Because the repulsed content is denied within our consciousness, it becomes available to project onto others.

When a strong repulsion erupts, it has a tendency to create obsessions. The person caught in repulsion struggles to free their mind from the chronic rehearsing of what he/she dislikes in another. The difference between repulsion and a dislike is a matter of intensity. A person can dislike a behavior or some quality about another person and remain emotionally detached. Repulsions pull you into a vortex of spinning criticisms, and the mind is filled with strong emotional attachments, no matter how irrational they may seem.

Marie the Workshop Participant

Marie was a frequent participant at workshops that I offered in New York. It became obvious to the other seventy-plus workshop participants that Marie had become antagonistic toward me. During the workshop presentations Marie would quickly raise her hand and begin her declaration with, "I disagree with you Father Bill…," and then she would repeat the exact words I used to explain a concept. The program participants were getting tired of hearing Marie disagree with me and then repeat the very same definitions.

After one workshop, one of the workshop participants who knew Marie decided it was time to name what Marie was doing at the workshops. John raised his hand after one of Marie's corrections and stated for all to hear, "Father Bill, I realize why it is important for Marie to correct you all the time. She is in love with you." The entire audience began to clap and echo John's remarks while Marie slowly sank into her seat and blushed in brilliant red. During the break John and I met with Marie and began to talk about her inappropriate behavior and why she had the need to publicly disagree with me.

In the discussion Marie admitted that I was everything she had hoped to become. She had a four-year college degree but wanted a master-level degree that would allow her to become a professional educator who gave workshops. Marie was recovering from a bad divorce that left her with two adolescent boys. As a single parent, Marie struggled for money and did her best to keep her two young boys off the streets and out of trouble. Due to John's declaration of Marie's unnamed and unconscious love for me, her projection, although negative and bordering on repulsion, was rerouted into a level of consciousness that began Marie's journey toward self-discovery.

In the monthly program that I was teaching there was an advanced training level for those who wanted to become certified teacher-trainers for the Healing the Family Institute. Marie was given a full scholarship and committed to the three-year program. Marie began to facilitate small sharing groups within the Family Institute and was very good at her facilitation skills. Marie was so empowered by her success at the Family Institute that she offered to facilitate an inner healing workshop at an all-women's college.

The president of the college attended her workshop without Marie knowing. She was so impressed with Marie's effective presentation and the positive impact she had on the women attending her workshop that she offered Marie the opportunity to become a part-time master-level student in the School for Social Work. Marie continued to offer the inner-healing workshops while attending college classes. Two years later Marie completed her degree and was hired to teach at the all-women's college.

Marie was able to work through her anger and jealousy at what I had accomplished and take her first few baby steps to begin her own journey of self-discovery. I am still amazed when Marie calls me and wants to negotiate definitions, applications and teaching strategies for her college classes. She is always enthusiastic and eager to borrow anything new that I may have discovered in the field of interest that we both share.

If a person's repulsion can be broken open and the underlying content brought to consciousness, a conversion from disgust, anger, repulsion, hypercriticism and a defensive posture can be turned into a positive working relationship that lends itself toward admiration, respect, mutual trust and deference.

Father Paul the Pastor

Father Paul was asked to be the pastor of a large parish church. This parish community had been informed throughout the past year that it would be unlikely that a resident priest-pastor would be provided. The bishop announced that St. Joseph Church would be one of the trial parishes for either a lay parish director or some form of a lay pastoral board. Parishioners were strongly divided; those against the idea of a lay parish director made their intentions well known to both bishop and parish staff alike. Those who were in favor of an experimental lay parish director or pastoral team were small in number but strong in conviction.

Father Paul came to this parish knowing little about the conflict between the two opposing groups. Patricia was a catechist and worked with the children's religious education department. Patricia was furious that Father Paul was the newly appointed pastor. She felt betrayed by the bishop's false promise of a new kind of lay leadership. When Father Paul met with the religious education team, it was easy to pick up on Patricia's anger. She was antagonistic and very critical of every suggestion that Father Paul had to offer on how to improve the religious education department. Patricia's coworkers began to confront her about her unchristian attitude and public disrespect and disregard toward Father Paul.

Patricia met with Father Paul to discuss her chronic anger and her desire to leave the parish and abandon her work with the children in religious education. Father Paul was both gracious and kind, and listened to Patricia's frustrated desires. With quality time provided for Patricia to explore her many feelings about her local church, the diocese, her marriage, her sick/dying father who lived with her and other personal struggles—a turning point occurred within Patricia.

She realized that her disappointments were not just about Father Paul coming to the parish as the new pastor. It was a culmination of life events that had taken her freedom to choose. Patricia realized that her life was more about surviving consequences than it was about choice making. With this new insight, Patricia began to see Father Paul weekly to explore her other spiritual struggles and concerns. Within a few weeks, her coworkers in the religious education department noticed the dramatic change Patricia had toward Father Paul. By the end of his first year, Patricia took the lead in creating a one-year anniversary party to celebrate all the good things that had happened to St. Joseph parish community since Father Paul arrived as the new pastor.

When cared for lovingly and with pastoral sensitivity, many people caught in the throws of repulsion can be turned around. Empathy, listening, attending, accurate feedback, probing, straight talk and tough love can help a person tangled in the web of repulsion become free and move into a conscious and authentic response. Turning the other cheek does have meaning when this very act of selflessness is used to waken a person who may be unaware or unconscious of their projections.

Managing resentful, immature people takes the same set of skills as raising kids: You have to combine the roles of nurturer, mentor and coach to succeed.[3]

Additional Resources

Consult the bibliography for complete publishing information on the following titles:

Jarema, William. *Conscious Celibacy: Truth or Consequences* (see section on infatuations, repulsions, fatal-attraction syndrome and sexual projections).
Johnson, Robert A. *We.*

Chapter 8
He Said—She Said—They Said
Patterns of Dysfunctional Communication

The skill and capacity to receive information clearly without bias is both an art and a science. Most of us average people struggle with the many filters we have collected that all information has to process through before we can make a summary statement.

This is what is meant by *filters*. You hear a statement. For the information to be processed in your prefrontal cortex with the assistance of both the linear left-brain and the affective right-brain, you will also have to manage how this information is affected by your personality profile (e.g., Myers-Briggs Type Indicator), your personal compulsions (e.g., Enneagram) and your leadership profile (e.g., FIRO-B Type). Then add in your personality weaknesses; your dysfunctional role in your family system; your undeveloped inferior function; your character flaws; and then your ego defense mechanisms. Now add a little fatigue, preoccupation and anxiety, and just maybe what you thought you perceived may be a little biased by the time you begin to organize your response to it.

Imagine, a person comes to you and their first few words go like this, "Did you know that John said he has some damaging information about you…" or "Susan said that Jim said at the council meeting last night that he swears he saw you with Mrs. So-and-So and the rumor is…." The brain goes into a state of alert, hormones are released that create a fight-or-flight response, your body registers a threat to be conquered or your heart, chest and gut become filled with anxiety and nausea.

In patterns of dysfunctional communication the bottom line for using such tactics is to offset the power distribution. The person accessing dysfunctional patterns of communication may only know how to communicate by using threats, sabotage and dependent or codependent strategies. As a pastoral leader, you need to make filtering a guiding point to empathize and understand the coping mechanisms of others so as to enhance your helping skills. "Those who have been given more—more is expected."

Functional communication creates an environment whereby two or more people can have their turn in expressing thoughts, feelings, desires and wants without fear of punishment. In the home, workplace or between two people in general, functional communication welcomes the process of exchanging information and provides the time, energy and attention to host another person's frame of reference. The effort to communicate well offers an abiding reverence toward another person, who speaks with words, gestures, inflections, tone and subtleties. The effective communicator contributes to the revealing of another by providing attention, presence, time, effort, energy and interest. The fruit of functional communication is known when another has encountered their "Ah-Ha" moment or has felt heard and understood by another.

There are dangerous and hostile forms of communication. Watch any television program and you will see how commonly known obscene gestures with clearly distinct messages are used with ease. Our world community has nonverbal innuendoes galore. Communicating through tattoos, body piercing, jewelry, certain brand-name clothing and nicknames can all communicate a clear message of affiliation and belief. In the workplace, nonnegotiable patterns of communication need to be declared. This means that the core values to be demonstrated and promoted within our Christian environments have been clearly spelled out to our primary staff, volunteers and pastoral leaders.

As the pastoral leader in collaboration with your staff, parish councils and volunteers, have you made your Christian communication values or nonnegotiable values available to the general church membership? Have you outlined what forms of communication are welcomed and which patterns will be corrected and challenged?

Christian Communication Covenant as a Model

Here is an example of a Christian Communication Covenant used at one parish and its school. The school's parents, teachers, principal, parish staff and volunteers were asked to sign it at the beginning of each school year. All agreed to promote the Christian Communication Covenant in every area of church and school life.

...if anyone is in Christ, he is a new creation.
The old order has passed away.... (2 Corinthians 5:17)

I am committed to these agreements in support of our community:

- If I have an issue, I will take it to the source.
- I will direct others' coming to me with an issue to go directly to the source.
- I will not assume your motives.
- I will check my perceptions of the matter with the appropriate person.
- I will communicate with respect, verbally and nonverbally.
- I will be open to receive correction as gracefully as possible.
- I will strive to trust and give others the benefit of the doubt to the best of my ability. [1]

Christian Response to Conflict

Glorify God.
Get the log out of your eye.
Go and show your brother his fault.
Go and be reconciled.[2]

Seven A's of Confession

Address everyone involved.
Avoid *if, but* and *maybe*.
Admit specifically.
Apologize.
Accept the consequences.

Alter your behavior.

Ask for forgiveness.[3]

Four Promises of Forgiveness

I will not think about this incident.

I will not bring this incident up and use it against you.

I will not talk to others about this incident.

I will not allow this incident to stand between us or hinder our
    personal relationship.[4]

Further Reflections

When I compare myself to another I diminish myself and deni-grate the other. God created each of us with specific blueprints that if honored and lived with integrity and authenticity can help us achieve holiness and become more the "image and likeness" of God. Every person has a gift or talent that needs to be encouraged and empowered. To live and adapt to another person's blueprints creates codependency and an inauthentic life belabored with worry, self-abasement and chronic failure to live life "to the full" (see John 10:10).

Jealousy: wants that which does not belong to me.[5]

Envy: a grudging desire for or discontent at the sight of an-other's excellence or advantages; to feel jealous of; pain or vex-ation excited by the sight of another's superiority or success.[6]

Jealous: demanding complete devotion and suspicious of a rival or of one believed to enjoy an advantage.[7]

Jealousy can be fatal to the life and soul of another. Each of us has a moral obligation to manage jealousy. Unmanaged jealousy and envy can become deadly vices.

Biblical Examples

In the Acts of the Apostles 5:17–18, the high priest and all his supporters, filled with jealousy, arrest the apostles and throw them into the public jail.

The Gospel of Matthew 27:15–18 describes the scene of Jesus before Pontius Pilate:

Now on the occasion of a festival the procurator was accustomed to release one prisoner whom the crows would designate. They had at the time a notorious prisoner named Barabbas. Since they were already assembled, Pilate said to them, "Which one do you wish me to release for you, Barabbas or Jesus the so-called Messiah?" He knew, of course, that it was out of jealousy that they had handed him over.

Envy and jealousy can harm physical and emotional well-being of those who sponsor such vices.

Envy and anger shorten one's life,
   worry brings on premature old age. (Sirach 30:24)

Whether he bears a splendid crown
   or is wrapped in the coarsest of cloaks—
Are of wrath and envy, trouble and dread,
   terror of death, fury and strife.
Even when he lies on his bed to rest,
   his cares at night disturb his sleep. (Sirach 40:4–5)

Be not vexed over evildoers,
   nor jealous of those who do wrong;
For like grass they quickly wither,
   and like green herbs they wilt. (Psalm 37:1; NAB, St. Joseph ed.)

A tranquil mind gives life to the body,
   but jealousy rots the bones. (Proverbs 14:30)

Exercises to Consider

Pick someone that has been your source of envy or jealousy.

1. What do you want from this person or, as you compare yourself to this person, what do you feel you are not getting that this person is?

87

2. In light of what this person has, is God calling you to accept the differences between you and the source of envy or jealousy?
3. Is God calling you to take the initiative and give to yourself what you envy in another?
4. Would you be living life to the full if you could access and integrate what you see in another person? If so, what choices must you make to begin living life to the full?
5. If you are jealous of another, is it time to make an offering of comparing yourself to another, thus diminishing what God has given to you, and stop negating what God has given to the other person?

Peter turned around at that, and noticed that the disciple whom Jesus loved was following (the one who had leaned against Jesus' chest during the supper and said, "Lord, which one will hand you over?"). Seeing him, Peter was prompted to ask Jesus, "But Lord, what about him?" "Suppose I want him to stay until I come," Jesus replied, "how does that concern you? Your business is to follow me."

(John 21:20–22)

When you take the inventory of another, their character defects, personality flaws, weaknesses, vices and dysfunctions, you take away the precious time you need to take your own inventory and begin to clean up your own act. People gossip, slander and defame others because they suffer from poor self-esteem, weak ego boundaries or frozen feelings; they may have a mother or father wound, feelings of powerlessness, allied themselves with the victim role or perceive entitlement without investment.

1. What do you gain by being preoccupied (exemplified by gossip, criticism, hyperconcern) with another person's business?
2. What qualities of your own unloved self are you noticing when you talk about another person's faults and weaknesses?
3. How can you broaden your capacity for love of your brother/sister when they irritate you or frustrate you?
4. How can you demonstrate this love so that your love can build up your local community?

Examples of Dysfunctional Communication That Are Harmful to the Christian Pastoral Minister and Those They Serve

Triangle Communication: An indirect way of communicating through a third person instead of going to the source. I tell John what bothers me about Sue with the hope that John will speak to Sue about what bothers me.

Top Dog and Bottom Dog: I put you down so I can bring myself up.

The Rescuer: Let me do the work for you because I can't imagine that you are capable of doing it for yourself.

The Perfectionist: I alone know the best way and the only way to get this done.

The Control Freak: I do not trust you to take the initiative. To feel safe, I have to contain and control all possibilities.

The Placator: Let me help you because I need to feel needed.

The Peacemaker: I am intimated by anger and conflict so let me medicate you with kindness and platitudes.

The Adaptor: I don't have a backbone or self-esteem or ego identity, so I will blend in with the majority. I have learned to adapt to and absorb he who speaks the loudest.

The Amplifier: If I repeat my message and speak louder, maybe then you will agree with me. Repeating the same words and expecting a new outcome is the prelude to insanity.

Conversational No-No's: These include the use of moral imperatives such as *you should, ought, must, have to, always, never, ever, forever* and *can't*. When I use a moral imperative I take away the other person's freedom of choice.

Name, Blame and Shame: When one finger is pointed at another person, there are three fingers pointing back at you.

The Mud Slinger or the Antagonist: If you say yes, I will say no. If everyone agrees, then I must disagree. If you do not listen to my ideas then you are stupid and blind.

The Victim: I never get my way. If you can do it, why can't I do it?

The Sky Is Falling: The three favorite words for this person include: *terrible, horrible* and *awful*. This person tends to generalize perceptions. If there is the possibility of a catastrophe this person can imagine it.

The Amoeba Syndrome: This person will declare that we, they, us and all of "them" think, feel, believe and want what this person communicates. There is an inability to separate the "I" from the "you" and the "you" from the "us."

Frozen Feelings and the Walking Dead: This person has the inability to self-disclose or reveal how he/she might feel about a topic or situation.

I Always Do It This Way: This person is like the control freak in that they are unable to adapt or cope well with surprise or unpredictability. This person believes that their template fits all.

My Way or the Highway: This person has a nonnegotiable communication strategy. Their pattern is similar to that of the top dog-bottom dog.

Threats and Gestures of Violence: This person, who usually has feelings of insecurity and poor self-esteem, will use cursing as a way to access pseudopower. Gestures of violence are used as a substitute for the inability to communicate true feelings and thoughts.

Workplace Harassment: Characterized by name calling, threats, forced exchange of favors, lying, secret keeping, gossip, slander and defamation of character, deliberate exclusion and discrimination.

Sexual Harassment: Includes sexual physical gestures, sexual jokes, sexualized words, pornographic cartoons and art, inappropriate touch, staring, a knowing violation of personal space defined by culture, offering sexual favors for work benefits, stalking, letter writing that contains explicit sexual thoughts and ideas.

Verbal Abuse: This area of abuse will need to be explored within a person's cultural and family frame of reference so as not to interpret cultural differences as abuse. For instance, some families with a large number of children tend to speak louder. There is more competition in wanting to be heard. Someone from a single-child family unit may consider this volume of exchange as yelling or shouting. Verbal abuse can include: yelling, shouting, screaming, raging, threatening, cursing, name calling, chronic criticism and berating, and a tone of voice that reflects anger.

Additional Resources

Consult the bibliography for complete publishing information on the following titles:

Crosby, Michael H. *The Dysfunctional Church*.
Riley, Mary. *Corporate Healing*.
Robinson, Bryan E. *Work Addiction*.
Wilson-Schaef, Anne, *When Society Becomes an Addict—Win or Lose? You Choose*.
Wilson-Schaef, Anne, and Diane Fassel. *The Addictive Organization*.

Chapter 9
Understanding Leadership Profiles for Effective Pastoral Ministry

Self-report instruments like the Myers-Briggs Type Indicator, the FIRO-B and the California Personality Inventory provide the pastoral minister and his/her team with a common language that not only helps each person grow in empathy and sensitivity, but also helps to create an understanding of the differences among people in the workplace. When employees expand their understanding of the differences among their coworkers, there is a reduction in misunderstandings and miscommunications. When coworkers become attuned to the particular and unique communication and work habits of one another, the team becomes more cohesive and inclusive, while exhibiting a pronounced improvement in networking abilities.

Naming patterns of personality can help describe coping mechanisms for conflict, anger and frustration: communication styles in matters of appreciation, mutual nurturance and support; decision-making patterns that emphasize either the impact on the group or the rationale of the decision; group skills for working well with large numbers or one-on-one; being inclusive or exclusive; and direct or indirect input to the work environment—all these contribute to feelings of empowerment, meaningful contributions to the workplace, and feelings of personal and professional respect.

Leadership profiles vary. Within your lifetime a pastoral leader may adapt and use three or four leadership styles because each pastoral assignment demanded a different pastoral leadership style. As creatures of habit, we pastoral leaders tend to specialize in one dominant leadership profile that stays with us for about seven to fourteen years. Due to age, health, maturity, workplace demand and life experiences there will be an evolution to everybody's leadership profile.

I have heard of some occasions in which people do not want to be boxed in with a label or a specific typology. I can imagine that with any profile misuse can occur. I have also heard that some people have completed one of the above-mentioned instruments and that their coworkers or employees could not acknowledge how their personal growth and workstyle changes had favorably influenced their working profiles.

It is my basic assumption that a pastoral leader not only needs to let employees, coworkers and volunteers know how he/she works best, but also to understand some of his/her leadership limitations. A personality profile allows for a common language to be shared among coworkers. When coworkers or volunteers learn of the differences between the pastoral leader's and their own leadership style, empathy and understanding can take root. Those served by the pastoral leader can also realize that he or she can serve a lot of people most of the time but not all the people every time. Helping staff and volunteers appreciate one's strengths and weaknesses as a pastoral leader is the beginning of humility.

The following instruments can be ordered through Consulting Psychological Press, Inc. www.cpp.com or 800-624-1765.

FIRO-B—Leadership and Interpersonal Needs

The *Fundamental Interpersonal Relations Orientation-Behavior* (FIRO-B) instrument measures behavior that derives from interpersonal needs. It provides increased insight into and appreciation of interpersonal behaviors. This in turn can lead to increased interpersonal satisfaction in working with or relating to others.

The FIRO-B is most commonly used to help people:

- Become aware of their interpersonal needs
- Become aware of how their needs may be perceived by others
- Identify sources of conflict with others
- Build more satisfying relationships
- Understand their own leadership behaviors
- Identify organizational culture and its implications

FIRO-B Assumptions

The FIRO-B starts with the premise that *"people need people."*

It defines *interpersonal* as any interaction, real or imagined, that occurs between people.

It defines *need* as a physical or psychological condition of an individual that, if not satisfied, leads to a state of discomfort or anxiety.

To avoid this unpleasant outcome, people are motivated to take action to meet this need. However, individuals vary greatly in what constitutes satisfaction and dissatisfaction.

Interpersonal needs can be summarized in three areas: inclusion, control and affection.

The California Personality Inventory– Biblical Leadership Talents

- Strengths and weaknesses of your biblical leadership profile
- Knowing your growing edge as a leader
- The Four Quadrants: Alpha, Beta, Delta, Gamma

Biblical Leadership Profile: My Strengths as a Christian Leader

Introduction

The goal of the California Personality Inventory is to assess the kind of everyday variables that ordinary people use in their daily interpersonal lives to understand, classify and predict their own behavior and that of others. Our application of this inventory is in the area of Christian leadership, since the talents derived from this inventory are found everywhere that groups and societal organs are functioning well as organizations.

Furthermore, we assume that a Christian leader needs to be able to do the following tasks in order to be effective:

ORGANIZE: arrange activities and roles of people, structure support, plan a course of action

DIRECT: knows how to lead people to accomplish goals; decides who must do what, when, where and how; motivates people

PLAN: predicts future events so as to utilize resources efficiently and effectively

MANAGE: can understand technical tools of administration, operation, accounting, evaluation, procedures

CHANGE AGENT: recognizing when change is necessary; the skill to satisfy unmet or new needs

We have therefore further assumed that to achieve the above tasks of a Christian leader, a person must have competency in one or more of the following personality talents or skills:

DOMINANCE   SOCIABILITY   SELF-ACCEPTANCE
RESPONSIBILITY   INDEPENDENCE   SELF-CONTROL
EMPATHY   NURTURANCE   FLEXIBILITY
TOLERANCE   CAPACITY FOR STATUS

The following descriptions of the talents as outlined by the California Personality Inventory are provided to deepen your understanding of your potential as a Christian leader. Your individual score is relative to the national standard, and variances occur within the range of each talent field.

This chart is taken from *Liberating Leadership: Practical Styles for Pastoral Ministry*.

The Four Leadership Styles: Sovereign, Parallel, Semimutual and Mutual

	Examples	Ideals	Characteristics	Relationships	Accountability	Support/ Supervision	Feedback/ Evaluation	Training
SOVEREIGN	*Traditional R.C. Parish (Pastor and Curates)	*Order and Obedience *Clear Accountability *Uniformity	*Authority Indivisible *Real Delegation Not Common	*Authority *Obedience *Dependence *No Peerage *Respect Rather Than Trust	*About (1) Obedience to Authority (2) Support for Agenda of Authority *To Immediate Superior	*Controlled by System *Often Not Given *When Given: (1) Informal, Not Built-in; No Forum (2) Mostly Pastor-Centered (3) Depends on Person, Not System	*Confined to Authority Person's Feedback *Based on Limited Observation *Judgmental (pass-fail) *Limited to One Person's Perspective	*Knowledge & Attitudes: Theological & Hierarchical *Skills: (1) Specific Skills for Ministry (2) Operating in Institutional Church *Role: (1) Competent & Reliable Subordinate (2) (Optional) Membership in Community
PARALLEL	*"Lone-Ranger" Teams *Hospital Chaplains *Military Chaplains *Academic Departments	*Smooth and Complete Division of Labor and Accountability *Autonomy *Responsibility *Diversity	*Task-Oriented *Real Delegation Common *Self-Reliance *No Consensus on Goals and Objective *No Joint Responsibility for Tasks *Little interaction	*Peerage via Isolation *Independence *Authority Divided, Not Shared *No Need for Trust	*Given Little Opportunity *Shows Little Recognition of Need *Sporadic *Problematic: Surfaces "Turf" Issues	*Hidden *None Built-In *Given Only in Relationship to Crisis *Judgmental *Vulnerable to Personality Assessment	*Hidden *None Built-In *Given Only in Relationship to Crisis *Judgmental *Vulnerable to Personality Assessment	*Knowledge: Specific Ministry (plus theological and hierarchical) *Attitude: Critical of Authority; Self-Sufficient *Skills: Management and Administration *Role: Self-Starters

	Examples	Ideals	Characteristics	Relationships	Accountability	Support/ Supervision	Feedback/ Evaluation	Training
SEMIMUTUAL	*Pastor and Board * Divvied-up Ministry Teams	*Clear Division of Labor *Some Joint Accountability *Autonomy Still Stressed *Coordinated Diversity	*Consensus on Goals and Objectives *No Joint Responsibility for Tasks *Periodic (not ongoing) Interaction	*Strong Sense of Shared Peerage *Interdependence *Authority Shared *High Trust	*To Self Only, for Tasks *To Group, for Plans *Self-Accounting Sometimes Reinforced by General Accounting	*Not Consistent *Restricted to Certain Areas and Issues *Implementational Tasks: Done in Isolation	*Inconsistent, Random *Based on Inadequate Data (no shared task performance) *Vulnerable to Personality Assessments	*Knowledge: Theological and Hierarchical: Specific Ministry *Attitude: Values Planning *Skills (1) Planning (2) Group Process and Group Dynamics *Role: (1) Source of Creative Imagination/ Change Agent (2) Formation for Teamwork
MUTUAL	*"Shared Ministry Teams"	*Sharing of Authority, Accountability, Labor *Autonomy Not Stressed *Integration *Diversified Unity	*Consensus on Goals and Objectives *Joint Responsibility for Tasks *Ongoing Interaction	*High Stress (periodic interaction without ongoing support) *Two Levels of Peerage: Isolated-Shared *Two Levels of Authority: Divided-Shared *Some Trust	*About Wide Range of Issues *To Oneself First, Then to Colleagues	* Built-In Systematically *Ongoing, Consistent *Both Formal and Informal *Given for Both Planning and Tasks	* Built-In *Growth and Development of Staff Shared by All *Performance Assessed *Supportive Climate Created	* Knowledge: Personal Development and Relational Dynamics * Attitude: Values Collaboration *Skills (1) Interpersonal and Group Dynamics (2) Theological Reflection *Role: Full-Time Team Member

Bernard Swain, *Liberating Leadership: Practical Styles for Pastoral Ministry* (San Francisco: Harper & Row, 1986).

The Myers-Briggs Type Indicator

Understanding personality preferences, the four functions and the four attitudes will begin the adventures into your preview of personality and your particular leadership profile. The MBTI will review the sixteen profiles and the particular strengths and weaknesses of each personal profile.

Explore the dynamic of Personality Type through the life span. Understand your potential and the ways in which your inferior function (shadow) reveals itself in interpersonal relationships, communication and conflict. God usually breaks through our inferior function in the dark love of desolation. Understand how to surrender to this unlimited gifted potential and move through the dark night by welcoming the grace of change and conversion.

Looking for God with our Dominant Function and achieving integration is the natural by-product of the growing awareness of our body, mind and spirit. Transitions are opportunities to usher in a period of integration, including an understanding of spirituality and how it relates to Typology or, as Carl Jung would say, "Broadening our spiritual outlook."

Understanding how Personality Type is experienced in Consolation and Desolation (dominant and inferior functions) helps us understand the human response to God's visitations and the consequences of those hairpin curves and unpredictable divine surprises. The MBTI will explore how to savor consolation and how to allow desolation to reveal undiscovered truths about your profile.

The Myers-Briggs Type Indicator can assist each of us in exploring how we experience play, work, intimacy, workplace contributions, leadership strengths and weaknesses, giving and getting nurturance and support, and how typology helps to achieve balance within our personal and professional lives. The Myers-Briggs Type Indicator can also help married couples discover their unique contributions to a healthy relationship, effective parenting and specific ways to improve communication skills.

How team members work well and the roadblocks they need to acknowledge can liberate a workforce to move beyond simple misunderstandings and become a more cohesive unit with empathy and understanding toward the unique and different contributions of each staff person. This instrument is a simple and effective procedure that provides a common language that encourages team-talk, teamwork and team cohesion.

Additional Resources

Consult the bibliography for complete publishing information on the following titles:

ADL Associates. *Back to Basics.*
Allen, Marc. *The Ten Percent Solution.*
Bausch, William J. *The Parish of the Next Millennium.*
Briner, Bob, and Ray Pritchard. *Leadership Lessons of Jesus.*
Buckingham, Marcus, and Donald O. Clifton. *Now, Discover Your Strengths.*
Bushe, Gervase R. *Clear Leadership.*
Callahan, Kennon L. *Effective Church Leadership.*
————. *Twelve Keys to an Effective Church.*
Engstrom, Ted W. *The Making of a Christian Leader.*
Faller, Tod. *It's All About YOU!*
Harvey, Joan C., and Cynthia Katz. *If I'm So Successful Why Do I Feel Like a Fake?*
Maxwell, John C. *Be a People Person.*
————. *Developing the Leader Within You.*
————. *The 360-Degree Leader.*
————. *The 21 Irrefutable Laws of Leadership.*
Swain, Bernard. *Liberating Leadership.*
Sweetser, Thomas, SJ., and Carol Wisniewski Holden. *Leadership in a Successful Parish.*
Walk the Talk Resources. *The Leadership Secrets of Santa Claus.*

Chapter 10
Safety and Security in the Workplace

This chapter is intended as a reminder to the pastoral leader that today the greatest risk to church members can and will occur while we are at public worship. Gather together a few hundred people who share the belief that we are all here to sing, praise and worship with good intentions. As the hundreds of people enter the inner church, notice how many exit doors there are. Has anyone prescreened the unknown worshipers who have joined us this weekend? Is there a planned strategy in case of a fire, medical emergency or attempted kidnapping? Are there security cameras to protect the offertory collection and its transport to another place to spend the weekend until the money counters come on Monday? What happens if a person attempts a hostile takeover of the assembly? Who does what? Do you have designated undercover police and security officers ready to respond to armed criminals who do not share your Christian values?

Airports have instituted a variety of security protocols so as to provide safe transportation to the millions of people who travel in and out of the United States. Large gatherings of people provide opportunities for psychologically sick people to act out their neurotic needs at the expense of others. Alarming consequences can motivate those with little morality and ethics to take advantage of innocent people. As church leaders, we must increase our capacity for safety and security for all ages in all areas of our church and school services and ministries.

The following are some ideas on how to broaden both safety and security for your church and school.

1. Gather a group of people who work for Child Welfare Services, the police and fire departments, alcohol and drug agencies, sex-

offender programs, the Environmental Protection Agency, and building and property departments who have knowledge about nighttime lighting for parking lots as well as security and safety standards for your church and school structures and grounds.

2. Have your staff, significant volunteers and worship greeters or ushers trained in medical emergency protocol.

3. Have a police officer evaluate your door and window locks.

4. Have you considered security cameras for your school and large program gatherings?

5. If you have an office and most church members know where it is, consider a front doorbell with an electronic buzzer and a preview mirror or glass door so that each person can be identified prior to entering.

6. Have all your external lighting evaluated by your local power company, especially the fixtures in the parking lots. If there is a dark area at night, this spot has the greatest risk of vandalism.

7. Do you have a curfew for all staff to leave the parish/school property by 9:00 p.m. and not to enter until office hours begin?

8. Do you have a policy encouraging all staff to walk to their cars with another person after dark?

9. Do you have a policy about minors meeting with parish and school staff after designated hours?

10. Have you had all your playground equipment evaluated for maximum safety?

11. Do you allow children and teenagers to leave the worship assembly unescorted by parents to use the restrooms? Are the restrooms in a secured and visible area and watched by designated adults?

12. Do you have a night security person to check all locked doors, windows, offices and storage rooms?

13. When a suspicious person is on the playground after school hours, do you have a sign posted that reads: "PLAYGROUND RESERVED FOR SCHOOL CHILDREN AND CHURCH-SPONSORED ACTIVITIES Playground use after school hours is discouraged. Nonschool and nonchurch members are in violation of private property."

14. Does your staff have a private/secret emergency button or phone code they can call if they are held against their permission?

15. Have you, your staff, leadership councils and significant volunteers reviewed the profile of special-needs church members so that a proper response can be given if needed in time of conflict or confu-

sion? Special-needs church members include those with physical impairments, such as the blind (visually impaired), the deaf (hearing impaired) or those who are wheelchair dependent (physically impaired). The elderly who show symptoms of dementia or Alzheimer's and those who have psychological disorders and may not have proper help with their medications may need extra attention during the worship service. Those who come drunk and/or under the influence of illegal drugs may need to be removed or supervised as long as they do not become demonstrative and disruptive to the general assembly. Is there a protocol set up for those who come to ask the pastor for money and/or food supplies and those who are verbally abusive due to a number of unmentioned reasons?

16. Who makes the first response when a person is disruptive while church worship is commencing?

17. Do you have an inventory of who has keys to your church, offices and classrooms?

Stories Embodying Safety and Security Issues

First Holy Communion Visitor

Father John was presiding at the first communion with over fifty young children eager to celebrate their first reception of Holy Eucharist. The church was packed. During the reading of the gospel, a young female woman walked into the sanctuary and took off her long coat to reveal that she was naked and sat in the presider's chair. Father John in his wisdom continued to read the gospel. He gave his homily, and then it came time for the Prayers of the Faithful. The children were supposed to come to the pulpit and read from where Father John had read and preached. He asked the music director to provide a portable microphone so that the children could stand before the altar. This way he thought, the children's backs were to the naked lady sitting in his chair.

While the children were saying the prayers, Father John went to speak to the naked lady and asked her if he could be of some assistance. She was clear that her intentions were to reclaim this building and this property on behalf of all the Native Americans who had been robbed by the white man. Father John smiled and then asked the music director, who was closest to Father John, if anyone had called the police. The music director assured Father John that the police were in the back and on the side of the church, and they suggested that as long as she remained in his chair that he should continue with the mass. If she became more demonstrative they would come in quickly and remove her against her will. Father John agreed with the plan and continued with the mass.

During communion time, the young lady decided it was time for her to dance around the altar while Father John and others distributed communion. After the distribution of communion, the young lady sat back in Father John's chair until the final blessing. Father John went over and invited the young lady to walk out with him for the final song. He was able to convince her to wear her long coat as they walked together arm-in-arm to the back of the church. Once they were in the back of the church, the police quickly escorted the young lady out of the church and to the nearest psychiatric hospital.

While downstairs in the community hall while the first communicants were eating their cake and exchanging cards, only a few adults who had seen the naked lady approached Father John. They asked why he did not have her removed from the sanctuary earlier rather than wait until the whole service was completed. Father John explained that the police were giving him guidance as to what to do and that he accepted their advice to continue with the mass and hope that the young lady would continue to sit in his chair. What amazed most of the staff and choir was that very few people even noticed the young lady walk up during the reading of the gospel. When parents were asked how they felt about what happened at the first communion mass, many of them did not see anything unusual. Some who were asked thought it was some kind of joke that parents were talking about.

Were there other options that Father John could have considered? Yes, they are numerous. Is the outcome favorable to your liking and expectations? If not, what would you have done differently? Do you and your church staff and leaders have a plan so that when such an event occurs, you know who is going to do what?

Sunday Mass Visitor

I was presiding at a Sunday morning 8:00 a.m. mass. The permanent deacon was sitting next to me, and we both noticed a young man walking back and forth in the rear of the church. This young man had dark sunglasses, a baseball cap and a trench coat. He kept putting his right hand to his nose as if he were sniffing something. The ushers, as I could guess, had invited this young man to be seated in the back of the church. He refused.

I leaned over to tell the deacon that in the medieval ages the deacons walked in front of the bishop so that if anyone attacked the bishop the deacons could offer their lives for his safety. I remarked that I thought it was time to reestablish this old practice. The deacon smiled and got the drift of my thinking. I suggested that if the man did not sit down in the back of church, to tell him that the priest sitting up here was going to take his cell phone out and call the police and have him removed immediately.

The deacon courageously walked to the back of the church and relayed the message. The young man admitted to the deacon that God had sent him to this church because he needed an exorcism and that I was to provide him this service as soon as possible. The deacon also noticed that the young man was sniffing a bottle of glue that permeated his breath and clothing. On his way back, the deacon went to his office and called the police. He informed them about the young man sitting in the back row of our church and said that he hoped the police would come, but without a lot of noise and fanfare.

Within five minutes, the police were in the back of the church. During my homily the police came into the main body of the church and quickly and quietly removed the young man. He didn't put up much of a fight or fuss. Later that day the police informed me that this man was seriously addicted to multiple drugs and that his glue sniffing was intended to carry him over until his next Social Security check came through and he could get a new supply of drugs.

Using the Washroom During Mass

Mrs. Johnson had five children. Her oldest daughter, Anna, was twelve years old. Mrs. Johnson was at a weekend mass alone because her husband, an army captain, had been deployed on a mission. Mrs. Johnson knew that the restrooms for the church were located one floor level under the main worship assembly room. She asked Anna to take her six-year-old daughter downstairs. Usually one of the ushers would not permit a young girl escorting a younger sibling to the bathrooms. This usher knew about Mrs. Johnson and her five children and thought that Anna could handle a quick trip to the bathrooms. This was a violation of our church agreement that a parent must escort every child to the restrooms. Anna walked into the large community hall that would then take her into the restroom area. She saw a man who immediately made her feel uncomfortable. She listened to her fear and returned to the church and told her mother.

The mother told one of the female ushers, who in turn reported it to the lead usher. The lead usher went downstairs with two other men and found that the unknown male, who was about forty-five years old, had hidden in the women's restroom. They were unable to restrain him. They called the police and made a report. When the ushers went to the police department on Monday to see if any of the pictures on file matched the person they saw, he was quickly found and identified as a registered pedophile sex offender.

Are your church bathrooms secured and supervised?

Is the room where the altar servers change secured and supervised?

Is the room designated for mothers/fathers with infants and toddlers secured and supervised?

Chapter 11
Evaluations

Some Do's and Don'ts, Supervision, Volunteer Evaluations, Peer Evaluations, Staff Evaluations, Volunteer Job Descriptions, Staff Job Descriptions

If you mention your idea or suggestion to a staff person or volunteer, consider it a small miracle if someone makes it happen. If you have voiced an expectation to a staff person or volunteer, you can hope that it is remembered. If you have given your idea or suggestion in writing to a staff person or volunteer, you can expect it to happen.

So much confusion comes from a lack of clarity between working teams of volunteers and church staff members. If you want to quickly resolve overlapping of staff and team expectations, begin with a review of who does what. With any good job description or job assignment given to a volunteer, begin with the basics: who, what, when, where, whom do we serve, volunteers needed, resources needed, accountability to whom and measurements used for quality job performance.

Volunteer Job Description Example: Coordinator of Church Food Pantry

Who Is in Charge?

The food pantry coordinator will be responsible to work well with volunteers who donate their time and talent to distribute food and commodities to those people who are preapproved by the local central food assistance program.

What Is the Job Assignment?

Be specific with each task to be completed.

1. The food pantry volunteers need to maintain a healthy and mutually respectful alliance and consult with the local food assistance program, the pastor and the parish administrator in all matters pertaining to the food pantry volunteers, the people they serve and the resources they distribute.

2. The food pantry hours for distribution are every Tuesday from 1 to 3 p.m. in the church community hall.

3. The food pantry preparation takes place every Monday from 1 to 3 p.m.

4. Volunteers may assist either or both on Monday and Tuesday.

5. Volunteers may not engage or offer additional support or assistance to those they serve, especially offering financial support, transportation to or from the church hall, or meeting with those served by the food pantry outside designated volunteer hours.

When Is the Job Assignment to Be Completed?

Can you specify from when to when? Daily, weekly, monthly or annually? Specify times and dates.

For instance, the food pantry provides food distribution every Tuesday from 1 to 3 p.m. in the church community hall. Food preparation takes place every Monday from 1 to 3 p.m. The food pantry will have priority use of the community hall, unless the pastor preapproves another church event. The food pantry volunteers will be notified one week in advance if their time allotted for the community hall has been cancelled, postponed or changed.

Where Does the Job Assignment(s) Take Place? Does It Take Place on the Church Property or at a Local Retreat Center?

This food pantry program is hosted at the church on designated days unless otherwise specified. For an emergency situation and with preapproval by the pastor, parish administrator or food pantry coordinator, food distribution can occur outside of the designated distribution day. This is to be a rare exception to the scheduled time for food distribution.

Whom Do We Serve?

The food pantry program serves those families who have been preapproved by the local food assistance program. Other families in need should be cleared through this agency, and only by exception—a preapproval by the pastor, parish administrator or food pantry coordinator—can emergency relief be provided.

Volunteers Needed

The food pantry program over the years has been managed well with at least five volunteers for the Monday food preparation. The Tuesday food distribution needs at least three volunteers.

Resources Needed

The food pantry program will need access to the parish community center kitchen every Monday from 1 to 3 p.m. Four long tables are required for both Monday and Tuesday as preparation and distribution stations. Only one door with a posted sign (Food Pantry Hours: 1 to 3 p.m. Every Tuesday) need be unlocked for entrance and exit for those families served. The bathrooms will need to be cleaned after the Tuesday distribution of food.

Accountable to Whom?

The food pantry program is a service of care sponsored by St. Bernard Church. The food pantry program works in collaboration with the local food assistance program and should follow all the state and federal laws and policies concerning public food distribution. The food pantry coordinator will review all monies required for purchase of all bulk foods and commodities with the parish administrator once a month. The food pantry coordinator will make an account of services provided and report twice a year at the pastoral council meetings.

Measurements Used for Quality Job Performance

The food pantry coordinator is responsible to encourage volunteers to work well together as a team. Serving families in need with a caring and polite attitude is the core value of this ministry. The practice of presence and patience must be constant because volunteers will experience the pain, fear and anger of people seeking food assistance.

Time Commitment

Volunteers are asked to make a six-month commitment with a willingness to seek their replacement from other church members.

The food pantry coordinator is asked to make a one-year commitment.

The pastor, with the pastoral council, makes a personal visit to discuss with the volunteers and the coordinator their perceptions of how well they are working as a team, areas of improvement, needs for assistance or resources and appreciation and validation for a challenging service program.

Staff Job Descriptions

If your diocese has an employee agreement or standard contract and job description for any of your part-time or full-time church staff, begin with that resource. If not, I would recommend contacting the National Association of Church Personnel Administrators: NACPA, 100 East 8th Street, Cincinnati, Ohio 45202-2129. Phone: (513) 421-3134; fax: (513) 421-3085; e-mail: nacpa@nacpa.org; Web: www.nacpa.org.

NACPA offers two resources that can help you save time and ally yourself with what is normative for job descriptions and base salary. The three "must" manuals for parish leaders are: (1) *Parish Job Description Manual*, (2) *Parish Pay Manual: Classification Systems & Pay Ranges* and (3) *Parish Personnel Administration*.

If you want to design a job description for a paid or nonpaid parish leader, here is a simple template to guide you along the way:

- Title
- Job Description
- Exempt or Nonexempt

An exempt employee is a full-time employee that serves in a capacity of an executive, administrative or supervisory position that is exempt from the provisions of the Fair Labor Standards Act. An exempt employee is hired with the specification that some weeks their job may entail more than forty hours per week. A nonexempt employee is paid a salary that does not include opportunities for over-time compensation for hours worked in excess of forty hours per week and holiday pay.

These church staff members usually work on holy days and holidays and are granted a flexible schedule so that if in one week an employee works beyond the forty hours required, this person can adjust his/her schedule the following week and work fewer hours. This is considered compensatory time and is not awarded on an hour-for-hour basis. Compensatory time is not a means to accumulate additional vacation, sick days or discretionary time off (DTO). It is usually the pastor or supervisor that determines the appropriate compensatory time on a case-by-case basis.

Here are some typical exempt employees who work full-time and who are not eligible for overtime pay:

- Parish or school business manager
- Director of music and/or liturgy
- Director of religious education for primary, middle school, high school or adult education, which may include the RCIA (Rite of Christian Initiation of Adults)
- Director of lay ministry and/or worship
- Director of youth ministry
- Finance manager
- Office manager if supervising other parish and/or school personnel
- Director of ministry to the sick, elderly and homebound
- Parish administrator or parish director or parish coordinator
- Pastoral associates

If the employee is nonexempt, specify the hours and days to be worked.

The nonexempt person typically has a job that can be accomplished within the amount of time designated per day, for example, employees hired to work Monday through Friday from 8:00 a.m. until 5:00 p.m. with a designated lunch from 12 noon until 1:00 p.m. Employees in a nonexempt status are subject to the overtime requirements of the Fair Labor Standards Act. When these employees are called to respond to an emergency after designated work hours, such as late night and special weekend job-related assignments, they are eligible for overtime premium pay.

The following are typical positions for the nonexempt:

- Accounting clerk
- Administrative assistant bookkeeper
- Grounds maintenance person
- Housekeeper
- Rectory cook
- Janitor
- Receptionist
- Parish and/or school secretary
- Volunteer coordinator (Unless full-time and work demands include holidays, holy days and weekends; then this person should be considered an exempt employee.)
- Food workers for school cafeteria
- Safety and security coordinator

Salary

Specific details and terms need to be clearly stated.

Benefits

Most dioceses in the United States have guidelines for diocesan health insurance, retirement options (like a 403[B] or 401[k]), designated days off that include holy days and holidays, earned vacation time, sick leave for personal and/or family care, bereavement pay and regulations, compensatory time or designated time off (DTO) and maternity leave.

In Case of Injury

Most corporations have a specified person that you must report to if you are injured or harmed while at work. With smaller churches it may have to be the pastor's job to be informed immediately if anyone is injured or harmed while on church and/or school property.

Sexual Misconduct, Sexual Harassment and Mandatory Reporting

If your diocese has this policy in place, make sure that you have had your employees read and sign the diocesan document.

Accountability

Each exempt and nonexempt employee must be informed as to whom they are accountable. Here you name the direct supervisor. If the staff is small, they may all be assigned to be accountable to the pastor. Otherwise, someone who may be a full-time administrative assistant, business manager or finance manager could be given the assignment to help supervise other employees. Even with volunteers, it is important that a flow chart of authority be specified so as to improve accountability and provide accurate feedback.

How Does Supervision Get Accomplished?

Each exempt and nonexempt employee has the right to know by whom he or she is to be supervised and evaluated. Clear guidelines are needed that specify how often supervision will be provided. What form of supervision will take place? Will there be a written summary report that both the supervisor and supervisee have access to?

Measurements Used for Quality Job Performance

In the area of quality job performance, it is important to specify how you will attain information that this employee is fulfilling his/her job responsibilities.

The following set of questions embody quality job performance. The emphasis on this measurement is that as the supervisor and supervisee each are looking for measurable, tangible and achievable goals that have been accomplished. Documenting the physical evidence is a primary goal of a useful job performance evaluation.

- Can this person embody and develop the parish vision and/or mission statement?
- Does this person have skills for inclusion of volunteers, youth, seniors and/or other specialized groups in the parish?
- Will there be a six-month or annual review of this person's job description and measurement(s) for quality job performance?
- Will you include a peer-staff evaluation process?
- Will you include any parish membership evaluation process?
- Will the staff person be asked to evaluate their perceived job performance?

Evaluations and Measurements Used for Volunteers

The reward for most volunteers is the shared appreciation of making a meaningful contribution for the good of the overall church membership and mission. Volunteers come for many different reasons. So that a proper measurement can be used to ascertain the quality of a volunteer's job performance, the following need to be defined: level of impact, engagement, teamwork and effectiveness.

Marge is the coordinator of the Fall Festival, which happens every year the last weekend of September. She has a team of over three hundred volunteers who contribute to the food booths, the arts and crafts, the general raffle and the other six raffles sponsored by various school and church organizations, the children's games, the public and silent auction and the music program.

The core team has worked together for about ten years. Each core member has an area of specialty and a primary job to promote and include as many other church members as possible throughout the eight-month preparation period.

The core team has had new members every year. New ideas and suggestions occur at a brainstorming session that Marge hosts prior to the beginning of the intense preparation period. Not all suggestions become a new addition to the Fall Festival. The core team has had years of experience in gathering knowledge of what people like and what they do not like at this annual event.

The job description for the Fall Festival Coordinator has specific times and dates of goals that must be accomplished for this enormous activity to take place. Marge spends time twice a month speaking from the pulpit, announcing upcoming planning groups, and invites the entire parish membership to volunteer. Some of the planning groups make arts and crafts that are sold at the Fall Festival. Other planning groups make specialized food products like egg rolls, pierogi and specialty breads.

The team that promotes and sells the general raffle tickets and the other specialty raffle tickets begins about three months before the actual date of the Fall Festival.

The pastor and his leadership council have specified the measurements for quality of job performance for Marge and her core team, as well as, the participants of the smaller planning sessions.

Measurements for Quality Job Performance

Inclusion: How many people did you personally invite to share in this parish activity?

Joy: Did your volunteers have a good time and was there a presence of laughter and good cheer among your coworkers?

Meaningful Contribution(s): Did your volunteers communicate that their time and talents were well used in this volunteer activity? Are there areas for improvement if volunteers returned next year to help?

Moments of Mercy: How did your volunteer contribution make you more aware of becoming a generous distributor of mercy? Did you have a moment of gratitude or an encounter with another person that brightened your awareness of God's presence in your life?

After-Action Summary Report

An after-action summary report is most important from one event to the next so that the lessons learned in preparing for a parish event do not have to be reinvented. The lead coordinator of every parish activity should have this as a primary responsibility in his or her job description so that the after-action report becomes a book of guidance for the next generation.

The following list offers some ideas to include in your after-action report:

- Document all the names and phone numbers of the Fall Festival core team and their respective small planning teams.
- List all the places that provided and donated resources. Who are some of your significant contacts or businesses that either donated or made partial contributions such as printing flyers and raffle tickets, or provided advertisements or resources needed for any activities of the Fall Festival? This also helps with sending thank-you notes to the right people.
- List all the rules and guidelines for parish raffles and public and private auctions.
- Include reminders for next year's planning sessions: Is there a need for more or less resources for the next program?
- Were there issues and concerns that need to be remembered from one year to the next?
- What areas of improvement have been suggested?
- Include a summary sheet of funds spent and money earned for general publication so that the whole parish can celebrate.
- Comprise a summary report describing how the Fall Festival coordinator, core team and small planning groups, with other volunteers, demonstrated the measurements for quality of job performance.

Peer Evaluation for Volunteers and/or Church Staff

[For the sake of clarity I will refer to church staff throughout my explanation of the peer evaluation, knowing that a pastor could use this evaluation procedure with volunteers, council leaders and committee chairpersons.]

The peer evaluation invites feedback from church members and church staff who have direct contact with the person being evaluated.

Some Guidelines for Using the Peer Evaluation:

1. Request that the person to be evaluated invite three people they either serve or work with to complete the evaluation form. Then have the person to be evaluated ask one or two staff members or other volunteers to evaluate them.

2. The pastor should invite three other people from the parish at large who have had some direct contact with the person to be evaluated to complete the evaluation form. Ideally, the pastor would also ask one or two other staff members to contribute to the evaluation. If by chance the pastor asks a person already selected by the church staff member, select another person. The evaluation process is not to be seen as secretive or anonymous—rather, as the body of Christ, we are attempting to build one another up by looking for potential ways to grow and improve in areas of service and ministry.

3. The pastor collects all the evaluations. Each evaluation must be signed. Each person contributing to the evaluation process must be willing to discuss any and all critical items with the pastor. The review and understanding of suggestions made are to help the pastor provide a useful evaluation experience so that the church staff member can feel appreciated, strengths and effectiveness validated, and areas of improvement named. The peer evaluation information will help the pastor, along with the church staff member, create an action plan for personal and professional growth using the feedback provided by each person's evaluation. The pastor will benefit from the peer evaluation in that it will contribute to his/her ability in objectively negotiating not only the changes needed for each church staff person, but also those relating to his/her department and areas of responsibility.

4. The summary report is a synthesis of feedback provided by each of the evaluations. The pastor will find it helpful to synthesize the specific remarks and put them on a separate report form while keeping the name of the evaluation provider anonymous. A review of the summary report belongs to the pastor and church staff member.

Peer Evaluation Form

The purpose of this evaluation is to provide helpful and useful feedback for the following church staff member: _____.

Please be specific in your comments and make suggestions that could help this staff person become more confident and effective in their area of service and ministry. Your signature guarantees that your feedback will be added to the overall evaluations summary report. Your name will not be disclosed to the person being evaluated. Your signature allows the pastor to contact you if he/she needs clarification for any of your suggestions made on the peer evaluation report. *For the complete form, see online handout 1, Peer Evaluation Form.*

To access the handouts, go to www.paulistpress.com, select Online Resources, and then select the book title, *A Survival Guide for Church Ministers.*

Pastor's Evaluation of Church Staff Member

Name of church staff member: _____

Date of evaluation: _____

Evaluation period includes the following amount of time:

_____

Scale 1 = Below Average Performance—Needs Significant Improvement

Scale 2 = Average Performance—Needs Particular Areas of Improvement

Scale 3 = Above Average Performance—Areas Specified for Improvement

Scale 4 = Good Performance—Constant and Reliable in Most Areas of Performance

Scale 5 = Excellent Performance—Shows Mastery and Refinement in Most Areas of Performance

Circle which scale of performance you believe reflects this church staff person's capacity. For scales 1-2-3 it is helpful to specify significant, particular and specified areas of improvement. *For the balance of this evaluation form, see online handout 2, Pastor's Evaluation of Church Staff Member.*

To access: www.paulistpress.com, Online Resources, book title

Additional Resources

Consult the bibliography for complete publishing information on the following titles:

Blair, Gary Ryan. *Goal Setting for Results*.
Boyle, Victor J. *60 Winning Skills for Parish Leaders*.
Deegan, Arthur X. *Developing a Vibrant Parish Pastoral Council*.
DeSiano, Frank, and Kenneth Boyack. *Creating the Evangelizing Parish*.
Dubitsky, Cora Marie. *Building the Faith Community*.
Forster, Patricia M., and Thomas P. Sweetser. *Transforming the Parish*.
Gardner, John W. *On Leadership*.
Haughey, John C. *Personal Values in Public Policy*.
Hickman, Craig R. *Mind of a Manager, Soul of a Leader*.
Hoge, Dean. *Future of Catholic Leadership*.
Hoge, Dean, Jackson W. Carroll, and Francis K. Scheets. *Patterns of Parish Leadership*.
Katzenbach, Jon R. *Why Pride Matters More Than Money*.
Kouzes, James, and Barry Posner. *Leadership: the Challenge*.
National Press Publications. *Getting Things Done*.
————. *Techniques of Successful Delegation*.
Smith, Hyrum. *The 10 Natural Laws of Successful Time and Life Management*.

Chapter 12
Why Do People Gossip?

Great minds discuss ideas,
Average minds discuss events,
Small minds discuss people.
> Admiral Hyman Rickover, U.S. Navy

One ought to examine himself for a very long time before thinking of condemning others.
> Molière (1622–1673), Actor and Dramatist

No matter what anybody tells you, words and ideas can change the world.
> Tom Schulman, *Dead Poets Society*

Do all the good you can. By all the means you can. In all the ways you can. In all the places you can. At all the times you can. To all the people you can. As long as you can.
> John Wesley (1703–1791)
> founder of the Methodist Church

We can often do more for other men by correcting our own faults than by trying to correct theirs.
> François Fénelon

He who cannot forgive others breaks down the bridge over which he must pass himself—for every man needs to be forgiven.

> Lord Herbert

One reason the dog has so many friends is because he wags his tail instead of his tongue.

Unknown[1]

Freedom is the necessary condition of happiness as well as of virtue—freedom, not in the sense of the ability to make arbitrary choices and not freedom from necessity, but freedom to realize that which one potentially is, to fulfill our true nature.

Erich Fromm, *Escape from Freedom*

Anyone who refuses to admit his mistakes can never be successful. But the person who confesses and leaves them behind will get another chance.[2]

Hear no ill of a friend, nor speak any of an enemy.

Benjamin Franklin

The Power of Gossip

There is a story told of a new pastor who was forewarned about Mrs. Jones. Mrs. Jones had a reputation of speaking ill of most of the other church members, and she enjoyed any moment she could get to gossip. She came to the pastor and confessed that she tended to gossip but she did not see what was so wrong with this bad habit of hers. The pastor informed her that she would be given a two-part penance. After she completed the first part of her penance she was to return and receive the second part of her penance. The pastor asked Mrs. Jones to go to the church bell tower and on a windy day she was to release into the wind a pillow filled with down feathers. She was to notice where the feathers landed and report back to him for her second penance.

Mrs. Jones, on that very next day, realized that it was really windy, so she hurried to the top of the bell tower and ripped open the pillow filled with down feathers and watched as the wind blew them to every corner of the town. She also noticed that some of the feathers were caught by a gust of wind and were blown into the next town. She was quite proud of herself for noticing just how far and wide those feathers blew about. Mrs. Jones returned to the pastor and gave a thorough report about the wind, the feathers and the multiple directions the feathers took.

The pastor now gave her the second half of her penance. The pastor asked that Mrs. Jones go and retrieve all the feathers that she tossed into the wind. Mrs. Jones gasped and declared, "Why, that's impossible! Those feathers went everywhere and in every direction. It would be impossible to collect them now." The pastor shared, "Yes, Mrs. Jones that is what your gossip is like. When you speak ill of another you have no idea where and whom that ill-spoken thought of yours can end up."

Why Do People Gossip?

This could be a book unto itself. Put briefly, gossip has its origins in the following areas:

Poor Self-Esteem: A person who suffers from poor self-esteem feels empowered when he/she can berate and criticize another person—though it is done behind the back of the targeted person. The power play is, if I can put them down, I can lift myself up.

Comparisons: I can be just as good as this person. If I can convince others to listen to me compare myself to another person, then it must be true.

Sabotage: Usually a person who spends time gossiping wants a successful person to fail so that the successful person can be reduced to feel what the gossiper feels about himself or herself.

Triangle Communication: If I tell enough people about what this person did to me, maybe someone will tell that person and that person will come to me instead of me taking the responsibility myself for making first contact.

I want to be included: Some people gossip because they can vicariously feel included in the incident or action of the person they are gossiping about.

Projection: I see a person becoming or wearing out loud that which I cannot love in myself (so I will hate it in another—repulsion) or that which I cannot give myself (so I will envy it in another—infatuation).

Pseudopower: I can bad-mouth another person and point out all their faults and even convince others to believe my perceptions and see how powerful I am. Through manipulation and deception I can get people to believe my perceptions, which validate my strength and influence.

Getting Even: Revenge is a powerful drug of choice. A person can become hooked on the adrenaline surge that occurs when a person rationalizes, justifies and intellectualizes their aggressive and violent thoughts, words and potential actions against another.

Ego Blindness: In the absence of information the ego will assume the negative. The longer the gossip is maintained and nurtured, the more the ego exaggerates the initial perception.

Susan and Jane

Susan ignored me [Jane] *when I said good morning to her as she was walking out of the manager's elevator.* Within time the ego adds additional information each time you recall the actual event. (*Susan has ignored me before just like all the other managers—just like my mother has ignored me most of my life. Just like my ex-husband ignored me when I came to realize he was having an affair.*) Some of the additional information added to the actual event (*Susan ignored me when I said good morning to her as she was walking out of the manager's elevator*) may not have anything to do with the actual event. Instead Jane may begin to borrow from past experiences—even experiences and feelings unrelated to the actual event and person. The greater the value placed on the absence of information, the more intense are the negative assumptions.

Jane has known Susan for eight years, and they both began their careers at this megaoffice together as secretaries. Both have received small promotions and salary increases because they were productive and efficient. Susan had just completed her undergraduate college degree in business management, which put her ahead of Jane in matters of promotion to a manager's position.

A small misperception that violates a valued belief can evolve into an overreaction. A brief encounter with a misunderstanding can become a volcanic eruption with devastating and multiple consequences that could hurt and offend many people.

How the Misperception Between Jane and Susan Evolved

Later that same day while at lunch with other employees, Jane began to criticize Susan for being arrogant and forgetting that she was once an employee like the rest of them. Jane put the bait out there to see if anyone else wanted to join her hunting party. Another employee, Dave, was overlooked a third time for a promotion. He believed he should have received a promotion before Susan received hers. Dave joined in on the gossip and defamation of character. Dave said, "Yeah, Susan is just like the rest of those who got promotions. They forget that they got their promotions because the rest of us make them look good."

While bad-mouthing Susan, Jane looked up and sneered at Susan who was walking toward them. Susan sat next to Jane and asked, "You don't look so happy today, Jane. What's up?"

Jane included Dave in her retort, "Oh, Dave and I have been talking about people who get promotions and how their entire personality changes for the worst."

Susan looked stunned, "Why would you say such a thing, Jane?"

Jane replied, "Just like you to avoid any fault, Susan! Now that you are promoted, you stand above all the rest of us."

Susan became aware that something had happened to Jane and wanted to investigate this further. Susan refused to argue with Jane and became empathetic and broke through the wall of camouflage that Jane was using.

Susan turned and looked straight into Jane's eyes and asked, "Jane, what did I do that makes you so angry with me?"

Jane recounted how she had greeted Susan while coming out of the manager's elevator and that Susan had not acknowledged Jane. Jane admitted that she felt embarrassed and that the other employees teased her about how she is now on a lower rung of the ladder than Susan. Jane felt hurt and betrayed by Susan.

Susan tried to remember if she had heard or seen Jane that morning and recounted to Jane, "Jane, were you aware of the volume of noise that came out of the elevator. Everyone was talking. There had to be at least twenty managers walking out together. I did notice another large group of people heading toward the workroom. So with about thirty-five people all talking, did you notice that I was struggling with my cell phone? I was trying to speak to my husband who is home with the flu. You know that when he gets sick he is such a big baby. I was making arrangements for my sister to pick up the kids after school with the hope that she would keep them at her house until I could pick them up after work. You are probably correct in that I did not hear you welcome me this morning. But for a moment, enter my frame of reference. A large crowd in the elevator, everyone talking all at once, me on my cell phone with my sick husband and another large crowd talking who are surrounding you while every one of us are walking into the workroom. So what do you think now about my not hearing you greet me this morning?"

Jane blushed and immediately apologized for her reaction to Susan. Jane felt embarrassed by her overreaction and how quickly she was willing to speak ill of someone she had known for years. Jane offered her apology and agreed that her expectations were unfair in spite of Susan's situation.

Susan was kind enough to accept Jane's apology and reassured Jane that her day for a promotion would happen.

Susan then looked at Dave and explained, "All the managers would agree with you, Dave, that our success is completely dependent on the success of all the workers we help and assist. Without good workers like you and Jane we could not be as successful as we are as a company. I suggest that instead of licking your wounds for not getting promoted, you may want to ask your supervisor what you could do better or differently to get a promotion next time your name comes around. This company is looking for managers who will go the extra mile. I did. I went to night school while juggling three children, a husband and a household. My degree was what I needed to get my promotion. And by the way, Dave and Jane, have you noticed that I am the only manager sitting with previous friends who I worked with prior to my promotion? Look around. You won't see other managers sitting with lower-ranking employees. I have been told that if I want to climb the ladder I have to hang out with the "big dogs," which means other managers or upper supervisors. Actually, I enjoy your company and would like to know that you are still my friends."

Susan provided a great lesson for Jane and Dave: straight talk and tough love. Susan was willing to put her immediate feelings aside and became the investigator to help Jane discover what it was that she felt she lost and how they could both negotiate their differences.

Additional Resources

Consult the bibliography for complete publishing information on the following titles:

Hackman, Michael Z., and Craig E. Johnson. *Leadership, A Communication Perspective*.
Hinnebusch, Paul. *The Beatitudes: Seeking the Joy of God's Kingdom*.
National Press Publications. *How to Manage Conflict*.
————. *Positive Performance Management*.
————. *Team Building*.
Wilkes, Paul. *Excellent Catholic Parishes*.
Winseman, Albert L., Donald O. Clifton, and Curt Liesveld. *Living Your Strengths*.

Chapter 13
Counseling and Spiritual Direction
Do's and Don'ts

Today men and women are trained, supervised and licensed with an ongoing requirement of continuing education and training to maintain a professional certification and/or license. The minimum requirement for most licensed professionals assumes a master-level degree. To earn such a degree, including the added requirements of additional supervision to achieve advanced certifications and ongoing recertification, makes the helping profession competitive. The financial investments, along with the time and energy necessary to groom a person to become a professional helper, both add up to a major life commitment.

Clergy, religious sisters and brothers, ministers, rabbis and imams for many centuries have been the best educated and most informed about science, literature, history and interpreting a biblical way of life. Many church members have an intergenerational trust that encourages an open deference to their religious leaders. If you as the reader were to think back to the 1950s–'60s, '70s, even the '80s, most church members, when in need of advice, counseling or spiritual guidance, went to their local church or synagogue. The pastoral and spiritual leader was perceived as the expert in most matters of family, marriage, children, parenting and employments issues.

Today, not all of our pastoral leaders have kept up with the proper training required to hang out a shingle that says: *Counselor*, *Counseling*, *Spiritual Director* or *Family Therapist in Residence*. Unless you are trained, licensed or certified in a specialized field within the helping profession, do not promote a skill you do not have.

I was teaching a class as a part of the Mercy Center's one-year

126

spiritual directors' training program. Within our program design, students are reminded that the Mercy Center program should be one of other training opportunities that will give a candidate what is needed to become a really good spiritual director. Students in the field of spiritual direction training should attend a variety of programs and workshops that will contribute to a menu of appropriate abilities and techniques, enhance discernment skills, learn a variety of spiritualities and religious disciplines and read, read, read! The process of becoming a spiritual director at its best is an evolution and spiritual transformation that moves the director closer to God and deepens his or her relationship with God. Sharing this personal process of evolution and spiritual transformation is the privilege of an effective spiritual director.

Another point of conflict that has occurred worldwide concerns clergy and religious who claim that, because they have been involved in receiving spiritual direction, they are now capable of providing spiritual direction. I would agree that there is both a science and an art to being a good and effective spiritual director. Unfortunately, those who have had no formal training or supervision and do not seek ongoing education and formation in this particular helping field are at serious risk of doing more harm than good.

The chronic complaints I hear from untrained clergy and pastoral leaders providing spiritual direction include:

- Role reversal—the spiritual director becomes the directee and spends more time talking about him- or herself and their issues than the directee.
- Too much talking and not enough listening—the spiritual director dominates the session by talking, teaching, preaching and instructing.
- Giving advice—the spiritual director likes to fix problems, offer quick-fix recipes and gives advice to the directee.
- Overlapping roles—dual relationships can endanger the contemplative stance needed for the spiritual director to remain emotionally detached and open to God's movement during the spiritual direction session. I strongly recommend that the pastor or pastoral leader not provide spiritual direction to an employee or coworker.

- Confusing spiritual direction with supervision or counseling —the directee asks for spiritual direction as a disguise for seeking free and quick advice, passing on controversial workplace information, manipulating the spiritual director for personal gain, seeking approval of the spiritual director or disclosing personal matters that hold the spiritual director hostage because of confidentiality or internal forum.
- Developing inappropriate feelings and affections between the spiritual director and the directee—the directee creates an illusion that the spiritual director is the only spiritual guide that can be trusted and believed. Or worse yet, the spiritual director creates a codependent relationship whereby the director needs the weekly if not biweekly session with the directee so that their mutual adoration can provide the emotional fix they both need.

Example of This Illusion

I had a new spiritual directee who lost her devoted spiritual director, a priest, because of matters of sexual misconduct with another woman. She wept with a dramatic flare and confessed to me that her entire spiritual life was now in jeopardy because she no longer had access to her spiritual director, who was available to her 24/7. She wanted to know how committed I would be to her as a director and would I be available at any time to respond to her spiritual crises. It was then that I terminated our session and suggested that she work with one of our counselors. I explained to her that what she was describing was enmeshment and codependency that bordered on mutual narcissism and ego inflation.

As the potential directee was leaving my office she acknowledged that money was no problem if that would clarify things. Again, I reassured her that counseling was a better avenue for her to pursue. She turned around and wanted to know if she could offer me a hug so that she could feel my spiritual connection. I stuck out my hand and offered a simple handshake. She huffed and walked away with the closing statement, "Obviously you do no realize what a mistake you are making!" As she left the Mercy Center, I felt relieved and processed my encounter with one of the Mercy Center staff. I feared for the next cleric that this woman would try to manipulate and seduce.

When the infatuation between the director and the directee becomes inappropriate, this infatuation may lead the spiritual director to actions that violate personal and professional boundaries, such as allowing the directee access to private rooms in the rectory, giving keys to the church so that one's special directee can enter the church late at night for personal prayer and devotions, or beginning a sexual relationship with the directee.

Examples of Personal and Professional Boundary Violations

Mrs. Smith

Mrs. Smith would come to the home of Pastor Walter, where he maintained an office for late-night appointments. Pastor Walter used a room in his home for individual sessions with church members so that he could justify being home while working after his regular church hours. The pastor's wife and children complained that they felt intruded upon when some of the pastor's directees would ask to use the house bathroom or want a glass of water from their kitchen. What pushed the pastor's wife over the edge was when she walked into the master bedroom to find a church member sleeping on the couple's bed. She yelled out of fright. The pastor ran into the bedroom and explained that his directee was exhausted from the visions she had shared with the pastor and needed to lie down. He offered their bedroom. The pastor's wife demanded a quick exit of the church member, and came for both counseling and supervision with her husband the next day.

Sister Julie

Sister Julie was known for her empathetic skills and spiritual guidance. She had developed a large following of men and women who came to Sister Julie's convent throughout the day and night. Her house coordinator asked Sister Julie to contain her work hours and finish by 9:00 p.m. so that the convent doors could be locked. Sister Julie believed that her directees needed as much time as she could give them. The community members became concerned about how late Sister Julie was meeting with her directees. Sometimes it was noticed that she went to her bedroom after 1:00 a.m. Sister Julie was confronted about her overworking and her inability to set limits on her work schedule. Sister Julie admitted that she was emotionally caught up in one middle-aged man's problems and that they had become physically affectionate through hugging and kissing. Sister Julie realized that she had overidentified with her need to be liked and wanted, and had lost her own identity, which opened the door for diluting her professional boundaries.

Father Max

Father Max was a strong leader in the Charismatic Renewal and visited many prayer groups throughout the United States, providing workshops, retreats and conferences. Father Max ran a retreat center that offered twenty-four-hour adoration of the Blessed Sacrament. Only those who he discerned had the gift of intercessory prayer were given a key to enter his private chapel anytime, day or night. The same key that allowed access into his private chapel also gained access to his private kitchen and bathroom, both of which were next door to his bedroom. Prayer group members began to help themselves to Father Max's kitchen and food. In time, prayer-group members could be found entertaining themselves at all hours of the day and night. Father Max realized that he had created a false sense of privilege among those he preapproved to enter the adoration chapel. One night, Father Max was unaware that a female prayer-group member was in the kitchen at around 2:00 a.m., and Father Max, in his underwear, made his way to the bathroom that was outside his bedroom. The woman screamed when she saw Father Max in his underwear and ran into the chapel. Father Max had his awakening and renegotiated any further access to his living quarters.

Factors to Take into Consideration

Frequent supervision, whether it includes peer supervision with other spiritual directors in your local area or professional supervision with someone trained in the field of supervision and spiritual direction, is a great investment in protecting your ministry and career. Assessing your personal and professional boundaries will also help protect your ministry and those you serve.

If you are looking for a spiritual director, it is helpful to ask your potential spiritual director any of the following questions:

1. What formation program have you completed to become a spiritual director?
2. What is your experience of providing spiritual direction?
3. How do you continue your education and supervision for your spiritual direction ministry?
4. Do you have ethical guidelines that you abide by?
5. Do you provide a spiritual director's disclosure statement?
6. Do you provide a spiritual direction agreement or contract that states our spiritual direction relationship regarding time commitment, financial agreement and shared goals of our spiritual direction together?
7. Is your potential spiritual director familiar with the Ethical Guidelines published by Spiritual Directors International?

SDI Ethical Guidelines

Spiritual Directors International provides a list of spiritual directors that maintain active membership. Please note that Spiritual Directors International does not endorse or recommend individual spiritual directors. Qualifications of Spiritual Directors International members and all information found in the "Seek and Find Guide" are not verified by Spiritual Directors International. Spiritual Directors International is not a certifying body, but rather a community that supports spiritual directors and those interested in spiritual direction with resources such as educational programs, publications and contemplative practices. A directory of spiritual directors can be found at membership @sdiworld.org or 425-455-1565.[1]

As you read through the eight statements listed below, which two would not be a violation of credentialing or a contradiction of the role of a pastor?

1. "I am seeing my pastor for counseling."
2. "Our pastor is helping my whole family with counseling."
3. "My pastor visits my husband, who is in a residential hospice. He is providing excellent pastoral care for my husband."
4. "My wife and I are working with our pastor doing marriage counseling."
5. "I am struggling with depression, and my pastor counsels me twice a week. I couldn't make it through the week without his support."
6. "I see my pastor weekly for spiritual counseling, and it helps me while going through a really bad divorce."
7. "My pastor facilitates a weekly support group—men and women who struggle with eating disorders."
8. "My pastor cofacilitates a grief-support group with a social worker at our church every week."

If you picked numbers 3 and 8, you are correct. Today, there are master-level programs that will certify and license a person as a marriage and family counselor, a social worker, a pastoral counselor and a spiritual counselor. It is a fact that rural pastors are many times the only available professionals in the area for a married couple or family to have access to in times of trouble. It would be wise for pastors in those areas of the country that have few professional resources to create a viable network of professionally licensed counselors and therapists. If a pastor represents himself or herself as a professional therapist and harm is done to the client, "He/she who has title bears the responsibility and the liability."

Unless you are trained and certified or licensed as a professional counselor, make a referral. If you want to work within the purview of your Master of Divinity degree, offering pastoral care, a listening ear, empathy and accurate feedback, resources and networking, making proper referrals and consulting with other professionals are within your realm of training.

Otherwise be aware of the regulatory agencies that protect those who are receiving services from a certified or licensed professional. Listed below are the associations that can provide you with further information, legal and ethical data and resource people in your area. I begin with the American Psychotherapy Association and show you its

Psychotherapist's Oath. Ethical guidelines for most professionals can be accessed so that you as the client have a measuring cup for professional and effective services rendered.

American Psychotherapy Association

The Goals of the APA are to be the preeminent national association for psychotherapists of various disciplines: counseling, social work, marriage and family therapy, psychology, nurse psychotherapy, pastoral counseling, psychiatry, psychoanalysis, psychotherapy and related fields.

The Psychotherapist's Oath

As a psychotherapist:

I must first do no harm.

I will promote healing and well-being in my clients and place the client's and public interests above my own at all times.

I will respect the integrity of the person with whom I am working, and I will remain objective in my relationships with clients and will act with integrity in dealing with other professionals.

I will provide only those services for which I have had the appropriate training and experience and will keep my technical competency at the highest level in order to uphold professional standards of practice.

I will not violate the physical boundaries of the client and will always provide a safe and trusting haven for healing.

I will defend the profession against unjust criticism and defend colleagues against unjust action.

I will seek to improve and expand my knowledge through continuing education and training.

I will refrain from any conduct that would reflect adversely upon the best interest of the American Psychotherapy Association and its ethical standards of practice.[2]

American Association for Marriage and Family Therapy (AAMFT)

Marriage and family therapists have graduate training (master's or doctoral degree) in marriage and family therapy and at least two years of clinical experience. Marriage and family therapy is recognized as a "core" mental health profession, along with psychiatry, psychology, social work and psychiatric nursing. Since 1970 there has been a fifty-fold increase in the number of marriage and family therapists. At any given time they are treating over 1.8 million people. Three options are available for an individual interested in becoming a marriage and family therapist: master's degree (2–3 years), doctoral program (3–5 years) or postgraduate clinical training programs (3–4 years). Historically, marriage and family therapists have come from a wide variety of educational backgrounds including psychology, psychiatry, social work, nursing, pastoral counseling and education.[3]

How many times have you heard a married couple struggling with marriage and family problems mention that they go to their pastor or minister for "marriage counseling"? Church leaders have always been in a position to offer spiritual guidance, accessing both scripture and tradition to provide some assurance for the multiple issues that can affect a married couple with a family. Providing pastoral care is far different than offering "marriage counseling," which assumes a degree, supervision and licensing. Today throughout the world there are workshops and retreats that offer significant support to married couples, such as Marriage Encounter, Retrouville, Encounter Christ weekends, couples' retreats and Teams of Our Lady. These resources do provide support, empathy and shared life experiences that can contribute to a marriage and family in need of repair and support. For some married couples and families fine-tuning their faith and spirituality can put them back on the right track. Others may need further intervention with a professional provider called a "marriage and family therapist."

American Association of Pastoral Counselors

This association provides guidelines for a code of ethics, professional practices, client relationship and confidentiality, church relationships, interpersonal relationships, professional development, publication, communications and unethical conduct. In church ministry the title "pastoral counselor" has become all-inclusive. Volunteers can provide pastoral care without a college degree and state certification. The American Association of Pastoral Counselors advocates and protects the title of "pastoral counselor" to include only those who have completed a master's degree in pastoral counseling with advanced training and supervision. Pastors, ministers, rabbis and other church leaders should avoid using pastoral counseling as one of their available professional services. A pastor may provide pastoral care that might include some therapeutic intervention. The application of pastoral counseling assumes the blending of psychotherapy—therapeutic models to help mend and heal a person's fractured psyche and ego. Remind your volunteers to avoid using professional titles so as not to mislead those they serve.

The Association for Clinical Pastoral Education, Inc. (ACPE)

Mission Statement: The Association for Clinical Pastoral Education, Inc., is a professional association committed to advancing experience-based theological education for seminarians, clergy and laypersons of diverse cultures, ethnic groups and faith traditions. We establish standards, certify supervisors and accredit programs and centers in varied settings. ACPE programs promote the integration of personal story, faith tradition and the behavioral sciences in the practice of spiritual care.[4]

Professional Chaplaincy

In North America, chaplains are certified by at least one of the national organizations and are recognized by the following member organization of the Commission for Accreditation of Pastoral Services:

Association for Clinical Pastoral Education
Association of Professional Chaplains
The Canadian Association for Pastoral Practice and Education

National Association of Catholic Chaplains
National Association of Jewish Chaplains

In addition, whether in the United States or Canada, acquiring and maintaining certification as a professional chaplain requires:

Graduate theological education or its equivalency
Endorsement by a faith group or a demonstrated connection to a recognized religious community
Clinical pastoral education equivalent to one year of post-graduate training in an accredited program recognized by the constituent organizations
Demonstrated clinical competency
Completing annual continuing education requirements
Adherence to a code of professional ethics for health-care chaplains
Professional growth in competencies demonstrated in peer review

Hospital chaplains provide a significant contribution to the recovery and healing of their church members. The complexities of hospitals and nursing homes and hospice-care facilities demand that chaplains be trained in multiple areas of discipline so as to protect themselves and the people they serve.

The listed professional associations do not exclude volunteers who may provide a pastoral care visit to local church members and bring holy communion or provide a shared prayer or some other religious service. Pastors who may not be members of the above listed professional associations are not excluded from short-term pastoral care or spiritual care of their church members who are admitted to hospitals, nursing homes and hospice centers.

Lay volunteers who make weekly visits to hospitals, nursing homes and hospice centers should not call themselves chaplains. This title assumes completion of a graduate theological education with advanced training and supervision in the field of professional chaplaincy. A weekly volunteer is best recognized as a church volunteer or lay pastoral-care volunteer that has completed some formal training in providing pastoral care and spiritual care.

Those pastors and pastoral leaders who want to provide a more full-time and active presence to hospitals, nursing homes and hospice centers are required to complete a thorough orientation, if not some extensive training to inform them about hospital procedures, emergency-room safeguards and medical guidelines so as to protect both the patient, medical and nursing staff and other pastoral-care providers.

Why has this become so important today? Liability, health-care restrictions, client confidentiality, HIPPA (Health Information Privacy Protection Act) compliance, inappropriate intrusions, undue interruptions or medically/physically at-risk contact with the client, emotional violation or overstimulation with regard to in-patient mental-health concerns are but a few of the critical issues.

Examples

Pastor Martin

A minister, Pastor Martin comes to visit one of his church members, Martha. Pastor Martin is unaware of the physical restrictions that have been written on the patient's chart due to a recent neck/spine surgery. He is unfamiliar with checking in with the nursing staff for an update about Martha. Pastor Martin has instructed Martha that if she desires to worship properly with him, she would have to raise her arms in the air. Unaware of the medical risks and the list of physical restrictions outlined by Martha's physician, Pastor Martin helps Martha raise her arms above her head and causes Martha serious spasms and pain in her neck. A nurse walking by demands that Pastor Martin stop what he is doing because he is inflicting pain on Martha. Pastor Martin proclaims that the pain is just evil spirits leaving Martha's body. The nurse calls security and has Pastor Martin removed from the hospital. One of the acting surgeons was nearby and quickly examines Martha, discovering that two of the newly fused disks in her neck had been ruptured and that corrective surgery would have to take place immediately.

Father Joe

Father Joe was visiting a nursing home that had a mixed population of assisted-living residents, nursing residents and patients with dementia, different stages of senility and Alzheimer's. Father Joe did not take the time to meet with the nursing staff and get an orientation of the layout of the nursing-home facility. On his first visit, Father Joe met Dan standing at the inside of the security door. Dan asked Father Joe if he could assist Father Joe in finding each of the patients. The nursing home had over two hundred bedrooms and was designed for the safety and security for the nursing-home residents. Unknown to Father Joe, Dan was a highly verbal and functional Alzheimer's patient who has made many attempts to escape the nursing home. While Father Joe and Dan went from room to room, Father Joe enjoyed Dan's company. They spoke throughout the hour it took Father Joe to anoint and visit with each of the nursing-home residents. When it was time to leave Dan mentioned a shortcut to help Father Joe get to his car quickly. As Father Joe opened the security door with the code he received over the phone from the director of pastoral services, Dan asked if Father Joe could drop him off at the nearby 7-Eleven store so he could buy some needed supplies. Father Joe was duped. He took Dan and dropped him off at the local 7-Eleven store, not knowing he had just helped Dan fulfill his escape plans. When Dan was found later that day, his immediate family pressed charges against the nursing home for not protecting their father and allowing him to wander the streets without supervision. When the full story was revealed, Father Joe was mandated to attend the orientation at the nursing home so as not to repeat any further unintentional good deeds.

Pastor Rachel

Pastor Rachel was assigned to a large inner-city parish and was forewarned by the previous pastor that she would be called to the emergency room frequently due to the gang wars and the chronic street fights in the area. It was 2:00 a.m. when Pastor Rachel got her first emergency call. A six-year-old girl, Lilliana, was accidentally shot in the head and was not expected to survive the night. Her single mother had requested that Pastor Rachel come and pray with the family. Pastor Rachel parked in the chaplain's parking space near the emergency room. She had to complete the visitors' form, which is required of all new chaplains and by any visitor who wanted to enter the treatment rooms inside the emergency-room complex. It took about thirty minutes to complete the forms.

Pastor Rachel was about to walk into the small room where Lilliana lay in a pool of blood. Lilliana's mother was weeping beyond control. When the doctor began to enter the treatment room, he looked at Pastor Rachel and asked that she not interfere with the last-minute procedures that could extend the life of the child. The mother heard Pastor Rachel's voice and asked the doctor to let her pastor come in and pray with her and the child. The doctor yelled at the mother and looked at the pastor and said, "This child is not going to survive with your prayers. At best we can extend her life by an hour or so. If you want to pray, go somewhere else." He stormed into the treatment room with two other medical assistants.

The mother reached out her hand to invite Pastor Rachel into the room. Pastor Rachel hesitated and then walked into the room. She stood next to the hospital bed and spoke softy to the doctor. "Mrs. Johnson wants me to contribute to the healing of her daughter and to ask God to help you and your medical team do the best you can do. I am not asking that you believe or participate in our shared prayer. But I do believe that what I can offer is of value to Mrs. Johnson and her little girl. If you believe that my presence in this room, standing next to this little girl and placing my hands on her hand is putting her in medical jeopardy, I will relocate myself outside of this room. Is my request clear, Doctor?"

The doctor looked at her with eyes that spoke of fatigue and exhaustion and said, "Do what you have come here to do."

Pastor Rachel began to pray that the Divine Physician work through the doctor, nurses, medicines and medical procedures. Pastor Rachel held the little girl's bloody hand with one hand while holding her mother's hand in the other, and asked that God pour strength and healing into the little girl and courage into her mother, who wanted only the best for her daughter.

As Pastor Rachel continued to pray in silence there was a gasp from both the doctor and the nurse attending the little girl's bullet wound. There was a clang against the steel pan that lay next to her head. The doctor held in his hand the bullet that was wedged into the frontal cranium of the little girl. He looked at the mother and Pastor Rachel and said, "This is impossible. I don't understand how this can be. According to the X-rays the bullet was deep inside your daughter's prefrontal cortex and was inoperable. I can't explain how this can be."

The nurse lowered her surgical mask and looked at the doctor and then Pastor Rachel and then Mrs. Johnson and said with great compassion, "Sometimes God has other ideas in mind. Remember, Doc, we are just the assistants. God is the creator and has the final word on who goes and who stays. This little girl is here to stay." Pastor Rachel left after a few hours and was reassured by both the doctor and nurses that Lilliana was going to make a full recovery. They asked if Pastor Rachel could come back tomorrow and spend some time with Mrs. Johnson and Lilliana.

These stories are important to pastoral ministers who may not fully realize how important their work can be as spiritual-care providers for those in times of illness, disease and the dying process. That is why it is so important for pastoral leaders to learn and promote a professional standard of chaplaincy. For an extensive review of the role of professional chaplaincy and its importance in health care, please refer to www.healthcarechaplaincy.org.

Provided is a short summary of the ethical guidelines for a professional chaplain and the additional responsibilities that must be shouldered by those who want to provide excellence and effectiveness as a pastoral-care provider. Please take the time to read the full document, "Professional Chaplaincy: Its Role and Importance in Health Care" and prayerfully consider the challenges that professional chaplains are invited to meet head-on.

Professional Chaplaincy: Its Role and Importance in Health Care

Section 1: The Meaning and Practice of Spiritual Care

Spirit is a natural dimension of every person
Spiritual care: its relationship to health care

1. Health-care organizations are obliged to respond to spiritual needs because patients have a right to such services.
2. Fear and loneliness experienced during serious illness generate spiritual crises that require spiritual care.

3. Spiritual care plays a significant role when a cure is not possible and persons question the meaning of life.
4. Workplace cultures generate or reveal the spiritual needs of staff members, making spiritual care vital to the organization.
5. Spiritual care is important in health-care organizations when allocation of limited resources leads to moral, ethical and spiritual concerns.

Health Care Settings for Spiritual Care

Acute Care
Long-Term Care and Assisted Living
Rehabilitation
Mental Health
Outpatient
Addiction Treatment
Mental Retardation and Developmental Disability
Hospice and Palliative Care

Section II: Who Provides Spiritual Care?

Family members, friends, members of the patient's religious community, institutional staff members, local clergyperson, professional chaplains, religiously active persons and spiritual counselors.

Section III: The Functions and Activities of Professional Health-Care Chaplains

1. When religious beliefs and practices are tightly interwoven with cultural context, chaplains constitute a powerful reminder of the healing, sustaining, guiding and reconciling power of religious faith.
2. Professional chaplains reach across faith-group boundaries and do not proselytize. Acting on behalf of their institutions, they also seek to protect patients from being confronted by other, unwelcome, forms of spiritual intrusion.
3. They provide supportive spiritual care though empathic listening, demonstrating an understanding of persons in distress.
4. Professional chaplains serve as members of patient-care teams.

5. Professional chaplains design and lead religious ceremonies of worship and ritual.
6. Professional chaplains lead or participate in health-care ethics programs.
7. Professional chaplains educate the health-care team and community regarding the relationship of religious and spiritual issues to institutional services.
8. Professional chaplains act as mediators and reconcilers.
9. Professional chaplains may serve as contact persons to arrange assessment of the appropriateness and coordination of complementary therapies.
10. Professional chaplains and their certifying organization encourage and support research activities to assess the effectiveness of providing spiritual care.

Section IV: The Benefits of Spiritual Care Provided by Professional Chaplains

1. Supporting religious/spiritual beliefs and practice: These and other studies demonstrate that religious faith and practice impact emotional and physical well-being. Professional chaplains play an integral role in supporting and strengthening these religious and spiritual resources.
2. The importance of religious/spiritual coping during illness: Persons turn to spiritual resources during illnesses and other painful experiences, finding them helpful. Professional chaplains are trained to encourage helpful religious coping processes.
3. Responding to spiritual distress: Professional health-care chaplains play an especially important role in identifying patients in spiritual distress and helping them resolve their religious or spiritual problems, thus improving their health and adjustment.
4. Enhancing coping strategies: Persons turn to spiritual resources in the presence of painful feelings and experiences. Professional health-care chaplains are trained to help patients and families draw upon their spiritual and religious resources to cope with these feelings.

5. Caring for families: Families rely on religious and spiritual resources to cope with the high levels of distress during a loved one's illness. A chaplain's care for family members has a positive impact.

6. Patient and family satisfaction with the spiritual care provided by chaplains: Patients and family members are frequently aware of their spiritual needs during hospitalization, want professional spiritual attention to those needs and respond positively when attention is given—indicating that it influences their recommendations of the hospital to others.

7. Benefits for health-care staff and benefits for the community: During the turmoil of health care, decision makers are constantly searching for ways to provide optimal patient services within financial constraints. They seek to retain quality caregivers and maintain positive relationships within the organization and community. Professional chaplains respond to these concerns in unique ways, drawing on the historic traditions of spirituality that contribute to the healing of body, mind, heart and soul.[5]

Chapter 14
Seven Habits for the Effective Minister

The "Seven Habits for a Highly Effective Minister" could become a book unto itself. Many clergy, religious sisters and brothers, monks and consecrated lay men and women, ministers, rabbis and pastoral associates, full-time and part-time church workers who have made a conscious choice for working for the building of God's kingdom here "on earth as it is in heaven" have embodied these seven habits and demonstrate the importance of a chosen way of life. Whether we were attending a retreat, workshop or ongoing education, these "Seven Habits" have been mentioned as core elements to an effective ongoing spirituality of healthy church ministers. While you review these seven habits ask yourself how much time, energy and effort you spend on each of these habits. Can you admit to the daily, sometimes, minute-by-minute attempts to achieve an effective way to embody these seven habits? I have included some reflection questions to enhance your personal examination of consciousness.

Seven Habits for a Highly Effective Minister

1. Prayerways and Pathways to Holiness: Feeding a Hungry Soul
2. Spiritual Companions for Traveling Along the Way: Authentic Human Intimacy
3. Examination of Consciousness: The Ability to Ponder, Introspect and Confess
4. Self-Knowledge Is the Door to Holiness: Lessons Learned or Repeated

5. Being Used by God for the Sake of Another: Instigators and Mentors for the Salvation of Souls
6. Eucharist: The Practice of Presence and the Body of Christ
7. Redemptive Suffering: Finding God in All This Mess

Questions to Consider

1. Do you have a menu from which you can pick the prayer experiences, rituals and disciplines that will feed and nurture your soul and spirit? Do you have quality time for private prayer and communal prayer? Are silence and solitude part of your prayer life? Do you have a time and place to go where you are not the prayer leader—instead you are a participant? If you were to add to your prayerways can you imagine exploring new forms of prayer?

2. Authentic human intimacy and spiritual companions for traveling along the way are inseparable if you want to maintain being a highly effective minister. Do you have friends and/or family members who are your chosen companions for traveling along the way? Do you have peers with whom you can share your good and bad experiences? Is it time to join a support group that could provide you a safe place to become vulnerable and help you with your inner explorations? We are shaped and become whom we love: Who are your love investments? Do you have an exclusive relationship with someone you have to keep a secret? Do your close friends include your other friends?

See how many people you can add to each of the intimacy expressions listed below. Are there some areas of intimacy that show you have a strong social network to pull from? Are there some categories that have few people and need further development?

Intimacy Expressions

Instructions: Complete online handout 3, Intimacy Expressions. To access: www.paulistpress.com, Online Resources, book title.

3. Do you have a spiritual director or spiritual companion, a confessor or counselor who permits you to confess your weaknesses and talk about your inner struggles? Do you afford yourself the time and money to work with a counselor so that you can practice looking at your growing edge? The practice of "moments of mercy" affords each

of us the chance to ponder how and where we meet the mercy of God throughout the day. Can you share your moments of mercy with others? If you confess your potential for sin, it is unlikely you would commit it. Do you have someone with whom you can explore and confess your dark side and your potential for sin?

4. How much time and money do you spend on learning opportunities such as workshops, seminars, retreats, days of recollection, books, magazines, CDs and other opportunities for self-knowledge? Do you have the time and energy to explore, read and learn about areas not related to your ministry or work?

5. How do you respond to people you serve and help who do not offer any gratitude or appreciation for what you have done for them? When God provides you a chance to care for someone you do not like, how well do you cope? Who has been your mentor or inspiration for being selfless? How well do you reach out to those who are unlike you in thought, word and deed? Can people practice loving you in their clumsy and awkward way?

6. Are you at home with your own skin? Those who touched Jesus Christ were healed and liberated. What rituals of affection and what comfort level do you have in being touched? Can you be with another person in need and not talk or just be present? Are you quick to talk and give advice? When you spend time meditating who does most of the talking? God wants to pray through your humanity. What happens when God wants to pray through you with joy, ecstasy, bliss, laughter, tears, sorrow, compassion or contrition?

7. Is it all right that you don't have the answers to some of your family's and friends' problems? When you encounter mystery and God turns off your will, faculties and senses, are you able to trust and wait to be led? Do you have significant friend(s) or family members who can be with you when you are in pain, turmoil or confusion without shame or guilt?

Additional Resources

Consult the bibliography for complete publishing information on the following titles:

Baldoni, John. *180 Ways to Walk the Leadership Talk*.
Cook, J. Keith, and Lee C. Moorehead. *Six Stages of a Pastor's Life*.
Cottrell, David. *12 Choices That Lead to Your Success*.
Covey, Stephen R. *Principle-Centered Leadership*.
McGraw, Phillip. *Life Strategies*.
Templar, Richard. *The Rules of Management*.
————. *The Rules of Work*.

Chapter 15
Symptoms of Work Addiction

This chapter should be read in conjunction with the online handouts that are available.

Twenty Symptoms of Work Addiction

PHYSICAL SYMPTOMS
1. Headaches
2. Fatigue
3. Allergies
4. Indigestion
5. Stomachaches
6. Ulcers
7. Chest pain
8. Shortness of breath
9. Nervous tics
10. Dizziness

BEHAVIORAL SYMPTOMS
11. Temper outbursts
12. Restlessness
13. Insomnia
14. Difficulty relaxing
15. Hyperactivity
16. Irritability and impatience
17. Forgetfulness
18. Difficulty concentrating
19. Boredom
20. Mood swings (from euphoria to depression)

Are You Work Addicted?

To find out if you are work addicted, complete handout 4, the **Work Addiction Risk Test (WART)**, that will help you measure your work compulsion. To access: www.paulistpress.com, Online Resources, book title.

The Balance Wheel of Life

As recovering persons reorganize their lives to allow more space for growth, work becomes proportionate to life's other commitments.

Achieving and maintaining balance is the goal of those who want to develop their full potential. Work addicts are thrown off balance because of the neglect of other areas of their lives. If you want to move forward on the road of recovery, your wheels have to be balanced. We function as harmonious and whole human beings when balance occurs in four major areas of life: healthy work, family, play and self areas. The self area includes attending to such personal needs as spiritual nurturance, nutrition and physical exercise. The family area should include positive communication and communion with loved ones. Today's society has many family configurations, so that "family" means many different things to different people. Your family can be a spouse; it can include a spouse and children; it can include unmarried loves who cohabitate; or adults who reside with older parents or siblings. The play arena extends our needs for social relationships with others outside the family. Healthy work habits include being effective and productive on the job, enjoying what we do for a living, working moderately and giving equal time to other areas of our lives.

Achieving this balance is sometimes a tight-wire act. One way to view your life is to imagine it as a wheel made up of four spokes: *healthy work, family, play* and *self*. Each spoke is valued equally and gets equal attention if your wheel is to keep its shape. When one quadrant is unattended, the circle starts to deflate, loses its shape and becomes unbalanced and lopsided. Nobody is perfectly balanced, but the closer you come, the fuller, more centered and more alive you feel as a human being. And you will become a more self-contented person all the way *around*.

Taking time to develop a balance among all four areas of your life wheel will ensure more harmony within you, at home, at work and at play. To help you find the area(s) in which balance is lacking, complete handout 5 the **Life Inventory**. To access handouts: www.paulistpress. com, Online Resources, book title.

After completing the inventory, use the information to create your own **Balance Wheel of Life**. See handout 6, link instructions above.

Becoming more aware of how you think can help you find more balance in your life. Complete handout 7, **Managing Your Thinking Habits,** as a way to assess your general patterns of thinking. See link instructions above.

Chapter 16
Healthy Self-Esteem and the Continuum of Healthy Sexuality

This chapter involves the following handouts that are to be completed. To access handouts: www.paulistpress.com, Online Resources, book title.

- Handout 8: Negative-Positive Self-Talk
- Handout 9: Self-Esteem Inventory
- Handout 10: Continuum of Human Sexuality
- Handout 11: Body Self-Esteem
- Handout 12: The Serenity Prayer

Chapter 17
Ministry Burnout
Red Flags and Warning Signs

When church ministers come to the Mercy Center in Colorado Springs, Colorado, and begin their personal therapeutic program of recovering from "ministry burnout," it has become familiar for the staff providers to hear the similar signs and symptoms related to this pattern. Men and women, married, single or celibate, clergy, religious or parish lay coordinators all share common symptoms when it comes to ministry exhaustion and burnout.

Here are some of the symptoms the staff at the Mercy Center have heard from previous church ministers who suffered from ministry burnout. If more than ten of these statements fit your present reality, you may be suffering from ministry exhaustion or ministry burnout.

1. I feel tired all the time.
2. I find it difficult to fall asleep and/or stay asleep.
3. I drag my body through work most of the day. I just don't have much enthusiasm for my work anymore.
4. I spend a lot of time daydreaming while at work.
5. I feel ineffective and don't see much fruit to my work.
6. I feel unappreciated for the many sacrifices I have made.
7. I'm not sure if I want to do this type of work anymore.
8. I find myself angry all the time.
9. My church members are always complaining.
10. I can't stand to work with....
11. I have such strong feelings of resentment and anger toward....
12. I can hardly pray anymore.
13. I don't have a spiritual director.

14. I don't have a confessor or a counselor to share my deepest feelings about life, ministry and my personal challenges.
15. Where is God in all this mess?
16. My family and friends just don't understand how much stress and pressure I am under to meet everybody's needs.
17. I have not had a day off in months.
18. I can't think of the last time I had a real vacation.
19. I do not have anybody to talk with about my frustrations concerning ministry.
20. I have been over eating, overworking, overdrinking and....
21. I don't have time to exercise.
22. I get angry and explode over little things.
23. I keep fantasizing about early retirement.
24. There isn't much laughter or joy in my work environment.
25. The loneliness is killing me.
26. I have let most of my social network fade away.
27. I really have not kept good friends as part of my life and ministry.
28. I have no one or no support group to hold me accountable.
29. I struggle with managing my compulsions and keep excusing myself from taking full responsibility for acting out.
30. There is more discouragement and doubt in my feelings about ministry then there is joy or hope.

If you find that the symptoms listed above ring true to your experience, it may be time to find the right place and time to undergo an intensive period of reconstruction, redesign and personal renewal as a church minister. Most of the church ministers who have made it through initial formation and seminary and are working full time in a church ministry have heard about the importance of self-care, personal renewal, retreats and workshops, and of maintaining a prayer life that feeds and nurtures the soul. After a few years of serving in the trenches and the illusions of the ideal church, parishioner and church staff have worn off, many church ministers crash and burn before they even realize it. I have heard them say, "What happened to those ideals and theological wonders I was taught in seminary?" "Why aren't my church members cooperating the way I read it in the books while at seminary?"

The following is a brief review of the four phases every minister will go through during one's lifetime in church ministry. Each phase has particular life experiences that occur and contribute to the overall maturation of the church minister.

Phase One

For most newly ordained, it takes about three to five years to complete Phase One. This can only take place while working full time in the trenches. During this period of time, each minister has to learn how to negotiate the ideal with the real; theological truths and principles with pastoral applications; philosophical equations with human struggles and the messiness of life. During Phase One, research has shown that many ministers become so shocked and dismayed at the discrepancies between what they were taught in seminary and how unreal and messy pastoral ministry can really be that they leave ministry all together. In a study of newly ordained Catholic priests by Dean R. Hogue, there were two major motivations for leaving: the first was feeling lonely or unappreciated; the second was an event that precipitated a crisis of commitment.[1] Priests who resigned were identified as one of four types: being in love, rejecting celibacy, being disillusioned or rejecting gay celibacy.[2]

The more support a newly ordained minister receives from family, friends, minister support groups, bishops and the congregation members, the better the chance the newly ordained has in translating seminary training into church reality. Phase One assumes a period of unlearning "ideal applications and measurements." These include: the pastor is always available; the pastor is never unhappy; one has inexhaustible energy, skills and capacity to serve everyone equally all the time; theological principles and pastoral applications assume that one size fits all needs; the pastor's college degree prepares him or her to answer every question, solve every problem and be an expert in all related fields of the helping profession. During Phase One, the newly ordained or newly appointed church minister will begin to melt those nonnegotiable ideals with hands-on pastoral ministry experiences that shape and form more realistic, manageable and achievable applications and measurements of pastoral ministry.

Phase Two

Phase Two begins at around five to ten years of full-time active ministry. The honeymoon has faded and some bumps and bruises have been earned as a badge of honor. Some painful ministry experiences have helped create appropriate calluses that provide the buffer during periods of personal and professional frustrations and disappointments. Those who can navigate the stormy waters of ministry and sift through unrealistic goals assigned by church members, church staff and other church ministers will achieve a pastoral reality of goals and values that become a way of living, loving and being for the effective church minister. Accepting the awareness that "the church is a human institution divinely inspired" encourages the church minister in Phase Two to remain adaptable, flexible and accepting of contradictions while maintaining a positive, proactive and futuristic outlook as to his/her ministry adventures.

Phase Two ministers have established a rhythm and ebb and flow as one makes daily attempts to achieve balance and proportion between ministries and their related demands, family and other relationships, personal health care, prayer and spiritual growth and maturity, emotional catharsis and professional development opportunities.

Phase Three

Phase Three happens between ten to twenty-five years of ministry. The minister has developed ministry patterns and routines that have become well established. Success builds upon success, and the church minister has a firm foundation from which he/she can respond to the pressures and challenges of church ministry. This minister has collected enough life experiences so that hairpin curves and unpredictability are handled with ease. Prior opportunities have created a mental file of available learned experiences and accessible resources. The minister has a working knowledge of his/her strengths and weaknesses without feelings of shame or guilt. This minister can ask for help and network so that effectiveness of ministry application becomes a driving value.

As this minister reaches the end of Phase Three, a significant shift occurs. Remembering becomes a driving force for both prayer and defining the minister's identity. Storytelling and having others remember personal life adventures are a valued treasure. Reminiscing and savoring allow the minister to glean the wisdom of the past and prepare for a paradigm shift that will plunge the minister into a second birth. Some have called it midlife transition. Others have called it the second half of life. At this stage of ministry, what has been will not carry this person into what will be.

Phase Four

Phase Four is about treasure hunting. After twenty-five to forty years of ministry, the demand to begin an inner journey takes the minister into a sacred place that can be both frightening and exhilarating. This journey into the undeveloped and unexplored can be imaged as a journey through an underground labyrinth. When the minister embarks on this period of second birth, all that once fed and nurtured the body, mind, soul and spirit becomes sawdust. The transformation process of Phase Four is purgative yet promises periods of illumination. Letting go of the familiar and all that has been achieved through mastery and refinement becomes dust in the wind.

While the minister continues his or her adventures in the underground caverns of the psyche and soul, a refounding of identity occurs as each purgation is completed, so that what is released makes space for what is about to be received. Holding onto the familiar becomes blinding while in this journey of transformation. Welcoming the undeveloped, unknown and unexplored of inner potential invites the minister into a world of wonder and awe. Ecstasy and agony, bitter-sweet encounters, the dark night of the soul, God breaking through the narrowness of what used to be, all demand an inner renewal that will leave the imprints of those holy men and women who went before us on the journey and lived to tell the adventures.

While you journey throughout the labyrinth, dreams, imagination, visions, infused grace and numinous visitations occur that provide the directions needed to complete all the assignments that God has in mind for the minister in Phase Four. Prayer changes and evolves throughout our life. Rewards that once fed the mind and soul turn sour, and the search for new food sources is discovered. Values and goals of ministry evolve into something unusual, and family and friends begin to wonder if the minister has lost her/his way or mind. It is typical at this stage of transformation that creative expressions help the minister understand the new directional signs given by God. Art expressions such as poetry, music, dance, ritual, contemplation, creative writing, cooking, gardening, environmental awareness, all such ways of realizing and embracing the Cosmic Christ may take the minister beyond his/her church theology and introduce spiritualities that satiate this newfound spiritual awareness.

The minister in Phase Four experiences a wanting and longing for something more and feels the nudge to spend more time and effort with prolonged periods of introspection, contemplation and meditation. Prayers of remembering and gratitude break through the routine prayer disciplines. The minister comes to realize that strengths become liabilities. The time has come to enter a new understanding of identity. Personal and professional values change, and a new priority is revealed and embraced. This may take the minister into a radical shift in how ministry is accomplished and may direct the minister to leave what was comfortable and take on new challenges and different forms of ministry. A new spiritual awareness breaks through with a broader, deeper, wider and more cosmic awareness. How the minister embodies this new cosmic awareness may determine whether or not the congregation sees him/her as a prophet in our midst or as a madman or a madwoman who needs to go to treatment.

The legacy of ministers in Phase Four is a newfound excitement of passing on life experiences to the next generation. Giving away those hard-earned moments of wisdom becomes the elixir of joy for ministers who have the privilege of looking back to ponder and wonder on how generous God has been during their many years of serving the people of God. Watching others succeed in areas familiar and areas never accomplished is received with gladness and rejoicing. The Phase Four minister has had the taste of success and longs for others to enjoy the opportunities set before them. Celebrating others' progress and being present to those suffering in the trenches of difficult church assignments reflects the age-old wisdom of these ministers who value partnership, redemptive suffering and companionship.

Ministerial Identity Evolves

Each of these four phases of ministry development has multiple variations and pathways to be explored and a labyrinth of human formation to discover. I mention this so that you realize that ministry identity changes and evolves. The fresh-start minister needs encouragement to hang in there when ideals cannot be achieved. Making room for errors becomes difficult after ordination because our church and society have idealized the church minister to a fault. The newly ordained have some leeway when errors are committed if a forgiving congregation and senior pastor have had the chance to learn from their past mistakes.

If a minister has not had the grounding experience of being with a supportive and humble senior pastor, congregation or bishop, the foundation—or Teflon—needed to protect the church minister may be weak or ineffective. If there are cracks in the personal self-defense structures of the minister, advanced formation skills will be jeopardized. Ministry formation is a mind-set that reminds every living person that we are all students forever. Learning and unlearning are constant movements throughout the lifetime of every church minister.

Every church congregation needs a core group of loving and empathetic people who will provide the time and learning opportunities for the newly ordained minister to reconcile their sometimes unachievable ideals while enjoying those affirming moments of mercy that provide the truth, charism and love that cannot be altered in any situation. Hopefully the young minister will be given the chance to reshaped and refound ministry ideals while exercising personal and professional life choices. Otherwise, prepare for tragedy.

Ministry burnout happens. There are numerous reasons that perpetuate exhaustion and chronic fatigue among church ministers today. The evolution of the multiple roles a church minister must fulfill has become unrealistic and complicated. The demand for unlimited availability, inexhaustible helping skills and multitasking due to the lack of paid or professional staff are but a few of the universal reasons for creating a harmful ministry environment for church ministers.

The lack of financial resources or inheriting a church that has suffered from financial mismanagement can make or break any church minister. The pastor of a very large and wealthy congregation may find ministry easier than the minister in an inner-city church that must beg just to pay its utility bills. If you want to stress out a pastor, add the burden of an elementary school or high school with an older building in need of a major overhaul and a declining student population. Many pastors lose countless nights of sleep when the facts and figures no longer complement the present reality of church and school finances.

Most church ministers would agree that the multiple tasks of today's minister are never finished. There is a built-in repetition in the work of most ministers. One pastor told me, "Just as we finish planning Advent and our Christmas activities, the director of religious education and the youth minister begin discussing Lent and details that need to be planned for Holy Week. I realized that even before we could enjoy one liturgical season we were already planning for the next."

How do you measure the impact of a minister's contribution to the local church and congregation? Is he/she having any real impact on the needs of their church congregation? Making a meaningful contribution to the workplace is primary to any happy worker. If the church congregation is mobile and there is a high turnover of church members, the problem of impact and contribution can be amplified. In a similar thought, a church congregation that has little turnover and a history of members with decades of church membership can exhaust a pastor and use up his/her available skills.

Dealing with Expectations

Unrealistic ideals joined with the multitude of the congregation's expectations can be an overwhelming combination. Some ministry goals are inherited when a new pastor takes on a new placement. Because of the differences in leadership style, personality and work ethics, some of the previous church ministries and pastoral objectives may be unachievable.

Another significant stressor during a change of pastoral assignments is adopting the church staff and core volunteers who may have been working together for years and are not willing to adapt to a new pastor's leadership style. The minister who works with the same staff, volunteers and council members for years can also become exhausted and feel used up, dried up due to a lack of new ideas or an unwillingness to try different approaches to ministry demands. Familiarity can breed too much comfort if not paralysis.

Many church ministers abandon personal self-care and cannot maintain mutually nurturing relationships with family and friends because they run out of energy after spending a whole day providing for needy people. Each human being has only so much energy that can be used during a day's time. The minister who goes to work and depletes his/her entire allotment of human energy while at work will have nothing to share when coming home. It takes energy to exchange affection, pay attention to family and friends, live in community and be relational while at meals or shared prayer. If the minister gives all his/her energy to the workplace, coming home on empty creates a vacuum in personal relationships.

When the local church minister is expected to be on call 24/7, it is difficult to leave the "work persona" at work and come home and be at home. When the work cell phone or PDA goes off, the "work persona" and all its related stresses, anxiety and demands kick into gear. Being on call can keep the minister in a chronic state of alert and readiness.

The minister who presides at prayer and worship and leads the congregation in spiritual exercises and prayerful rituals may feel a deep need for quality personal prayer time and the feeding of his/her own soul. Leading prayer is not equal to receiving the benefits of being at prayer. The fact that a retreat director gives a good retreat doesn't mean that his/her mind, heart and soul are being fed and nurtured in a life-sustaining way.

Coping with failure, making mistakes and admitting weaknesses and limitations are usually not welcome material coming from the pulpit. When the leader of the church falls, some of the church members may not be equipped to provide support or pastoral care. Other church members will project their unresolved anger, grief or mother/father wounds unto the pastor for not living up to their ideals. Some church members will become punitive and self-righteous and expect the fallen pastor to grovel for pity or debase him-/herself so that those passing judgment can feel vindicated for their own unresolved failures.

Then there are those true children of God who have learned from their own sufferings that even the mighty can fall and be forgiven. Leaders are just ordinary men and women who have put themselves at the service of the community and have been entrusted to be good stewards of power, money, trustworthy in decision-making and striving to cooperate with the Divine plan. Those who have learned from the past are usually the most generous in forgiving and helping church leaders learn from mistakes made. Unfortunately, very few church members are willing to rise to the occasion when a church leader falls, wears his/her weaknesses out loud or shows signs of wear and tear from ministry burnout.

When most of our church ministers consider a new assignment, they will come prepared with a resumé of strengths, skills, past achievements and hopes and dreams for the future of the church they wish to serve. What if a new requirement was made for all newly appointed church ministers: an honest assessment of limitations and ministry weaknesses that will assume the support and loving care of the congregation. Successful church ministers and leaders are noted for what they can do that is usually extraordinary and above the norm of the people they serve. When excellence is the only measuring cup for any application of service for the minister, then pathological expectations brew and pathogenic attitudes infect common sense.

I had the experience of witnessing the installation of a newly ordained minister. I was asked to be part of his installation so as to contribute to the actual theme celebrated in his church on World Mission Sunday. I was part of seven other denominations that shared in this festive occasion. As this young married man witnessed to his congregation he began with a confession:

> Let me tell you about my weaknesses and what I don't do so well. I am not that good with group conflict and will need your patience and charity when big decisions must be made. I am overly cautious so as not to make big mistakes. I usually overprepare for classes and workshops and sometimes forget that the Holy Spirit may want some time to speak through those I serve and even myself.
>
> I am very driven to get things done and I tend to be a perfectionist. I will do my best to let others do what can be done in our church and call forth the gifts of others instead of my need to be in control. I tend to migrate toward those who think like me—so I will do my best to listen and include those who don't think like me or the mainstream talkers and workers of this church.

If I seem preoccupied it is probably because I have set up unrealistic expectations of my workload and ministry performance, and you may remind me to lighten up and help me laugh so as to enjoy the moment with you. Otherwise I tend to fret about all the things I need to get done and not savor what has already been accomplished.

I get excited about new ideas and new projects and can talk really fast, so if you are ever with me at a meeting and you see me running ahead of the pack, slow me down. I am very protective of my wife and daughter and love them so much that I don't take criticisms about my family very graciously. I like to work with my hands and be amongst the people, and I struggle to sit at my desk and take care of the piles of paperwork that I know are waiting for the pastor's signature. I will get to the paperwork, but I am easily persuaded to be amongst the youth group or senior morning coffee gathering.

I tend to overwork and overfunction because I accept my childhood wound of being an adult child of an alcoholic father. I attend a support group weekly to keep my own tendencies of codependency in check and my own potential for addictive thinking and feeling. I thank you in advance for forgiving me if I don't notice your affectionate gestures or words of encouragement. Tap me on the shoulder if I overlook your gestures of support instead of kicking me in the butt.

Thank you in advance for building on my strengths and having kindness and charity toward my ministerial weaknesses. I promise to give you my very best as your pastor while remaining a loving husband and father and protecting quality time with my family so that I can role-model for all fathers and mothers the importance of "family first."

Ways to Avoid Ministry Exhaustion and Burnout

1. *Maintaining fidelity to prayer and the spiritual life.* Seek spiritual intimacy with God and open yourself to having frequent encounters of

being used by God for the sake of others. Seek out retreats, workshops, seminars and spiritual mentors that can expand your capacity for spiritual growth. Explore a prayer technique or spiritual discipline and add it to your menu of prayer. Let God wow you when you make the time to dwell and ponder and practice the art of presence.

2. *Intimacy with close friends, family and, if married, your spouse and children*. Carve out quality time to feed and sustain these relationships by using time, effort and spending money for recreational experiences. Take the time to investigate some new adventure of play and recreation and offer your family and friends the opportunity to go hiking, biking, bowling. Try rock climbing indoors or play a friendly game of basketball, baseball, football, soccer or badminton. Making memories takes effort and planning, and will become the cement that holds family and friends together during tough times. How much time do you spend laughing, playing board games and cards, and recreating together with family and friends?

3. *Sharing quality mealtimes with others*. Make and defend the time to sit and eat and savor your food and share stories about the day. Learn how to cook and serve a meal so that your family and friends can taste the love you've added to your dining experience.

4. *Quality time off away from the routine of your daily ministry*. Each week schedule some time to change the routine demands of your ministry and do something unrelated to your work demands. Schedule an appointment with yourself for imagination time, creativity and daydreaming about your future and the future of the people you serve. Read and learn something that has nothing to do with your work and ministry.

5. *Breathe*. Every morning, noon and before you leave your ministry take a few moments and sit comfortably in a chair or lie on the floor and take some deep breaths. Let God wash away any tension in your muscles, carry any burdens you have attached to yourself, and surrender your efforts to a power greater than yourself.

6. *Practice the examination of conscience alone or with a significant other*. This is how you do it. By yourself or, taking turns with a friend, ask, "Today, how am I living life to the full physically? Today, how am I living life to the full emotionally? How am I living life to the full spiritually? How am I living life to the full socially? (Notice, the examination of conscience is positive. It is not asking yourself what you did

wrong or how you are not living life to the full.) The positive emphasis is to acknowledge God's graces and interventions throughout the day. You may replace this daily practice with a once-a-week examination of conscience either alone or with a significant other.

7. *Practice gratitude and look for the blessings in each day.* If you get the chance, it is worth watching the DVD *Celebrating What's Right with the World.* Dewitt Jones has named key attitudes that can help you achieve a positive and realistic approach to everyday living. His key concepts are: Believe It and You'll See It; Recognize Abundance; Look for Possibilities; Unleash Your Energy to Fix What's Wrong; Ride the Changes; Take Yourself to Your Edge; Be Your Best for the World.

8. *Be accountable to someone.* Do you have a confessor, spiritual director, minister support group, counselor, prayer group or a confidant who can ask you those probing questions about your life, ministry, and relationship with God, your family, your home, and about the sins and mistakes you have committed?

9. *Develop the art of self-care.* Are you a good steward of your body and health? Are you open to creativity and imagination, feelings and emotions, the spiritual life, the intellect and your capacity to learn? Are you exploring your growing edge in prayer, ministry, and your personal and professional opportunities for expansion and development?

10. *Receive from others what you hope to give in generosity.* The Society of Missionaries of Mercy has a prayer that speaks about the importance of receiving before giving. The Spirit Mercy Prayer said daily reminds these lay missionaries of mercy about the importance of being filled with mercy so that they can become generous distributors of mercy. Here is the beginning of their prayer:

> Spirit Mercy,
> enliven within me
> a willingness to be loved
> so that I may love;
> a desire to be healed
> so that I may heal;
> a longing to be embraced by your gentleness
> so that I may become tenderhearted;
> a wanting to spend my life in God's Kingdom
> and to become a generous distributor of mercy.

Help me to become a worthy vessel to carry
for others the oils of gladness and joy....[3]

All church ministers who want to practice a spirituality of longevity must learn how to let their guard down and open their hearts to the clumsy and awkward ways that our church members and coworkers will try to love and care for us. Giving puts each minister in the power position. Receiving begins by letting go of control, becoming vulnerable to another and letting someone else take the power position. Any minister who has felt the edge of ministry burnout will admit quickly that his/her capacity to receive has atrophied and that allowing others to care for him/her has become unfamiliar and foreign.

Broaden your capacity to be nurtured. Open up your options for personal and professional affirmations and support. Create a network of mentors, cheerleaders, advocates, advisors and teachers. If you look for the support and are ready to receive it you will find that your heart's desire has been within reach of your intention; you just were not ready to receive it.

I had visited a rancher who was showing me a well he had dug years ago for his cattle. As we arrived at the well we had to lift a large wooden circular cover so that the rancher could lower the bucket into the well and retrieve some water. When the bucket came up empty he turned on his flashlight and saw that the well had dried up. He looked at me and said, "Father Bill, this is a homily moment. You see what happened to this well? Because I did not use the water in this well often enough it had no need to refill itself. The well would replenish what water I would use. By not using the well water, it dried up."

If you do not use your capacity to receive, you may loose your ability to do so when you really need to. When you have discovered how to broaden your capacity to receive, share your wisdom with other church ministers. The helping profession, like church ministers, is about giving and helping others. So that your inner well does not dry up and you begin to thirst for the very qualities you share so generously with others, practice receiving. Dip into the well of love and care that others can provide. My prayer for all church ministers is, "May your well of life-giving waters never be exhausted."

Additional Resources

Consult the bibliography for complete publishing information on the following titles:

DeCarlo, Donald T., and Deborah H. Gruenfeld. *Stress in the American Workplace: Alternatives for the Working Wounded.*

Deci, Edward L. *Why We Do What We Do: Understanding Self-Motivation.*

Jones, Dewitt. *Celebrate What's Right with the World* (DVD). Star Thrower, 26 East Exchange St., Suite 600, St. Paul, MN 55101; 800-242-3220; www.starthrower.com.

Knell, Marion. *Burn Up or Splash Down: Surviving the Culture Shock of Re-Entry.*

Lehr, Fred. *Clergy Burnout: Recovering from the 70-hour Work Week…and Other Self-Defeating Practices.*

London, H. B., and Neil B. Wiseman. *Pastors at Greater Risk: Real Help from Pastors Who've Been There.*

Lucado, Max. *3:16—The Numbers of Hope.*

Perry, Charles, Jr. *Why Christians Burn Out.*

Sanford, John A. *Ministry Burnout.*

White, Joseph D. *Burnout Busters: Stress Management for Ministry.*

Wilson, Michael Todd, and Brad Hoffman. *Preventing Ministry Failure.*

Yager, Jan. *When Friendship Hurts: How to Deal with Friends Who Betray, Abandon, or Wound You.*

Chapter 18
Stewardship
Responding to God's Generosity

Being a good Christian steward involves at least these three responsibilities:

1. The wide use of God's gifts and resources, which means taking good care of ourselves and our environment.
2. The use of our talents and skills in a manner that is pleasing to God and consistent with Gospel values.
3. Gratefully returning a portion of God's resources—our time, talent and treasure—for God's work in the world.[1]

Today many churches are merging due to a shift in demographics or an aging population. "Cluster" churches are being formed so that centralized staff; parish programs and a shared pastor are the expected norm. Pastors are now being asked to supervise multiple churches due to the decline of vocations to ministry, whether it be pastorship, the priesthood or religious life. And with the aging of our present clergy and religious, no wonder, that "time has replaced gold as our most precious commodity."[2] How a church leader manages their stewardship of time can make or break his or her health, career and family. Each church leader must take an inventory of one's own stewardship of time. Making the time for the art of self-care is a nonnegotiable. For those who want to celebrate a spirituality of longevity, taking the time to discover the resources that can nurture and refresh the church leader is a matter of life or death. Each steward called by God is "one who receives God's gifts gratefully, cherishes and tends them in a responsible and accountable manner, shares them in justice and love with others, and returns them with increase to the Lord."[3]

Four Fundamental Values of Stewardship

Core to a stewardship way of life are four fundamental values. The first is accepting and promoting the process of conversion within our self that welcomes innovations and embraces the necessary changes to move deeper into the mystery of "…God as the origin of life, the giver of freedom, the source of all they have and are and will be."[4] Reflecting on the Torah-based approach to environmental stewardship, the Acton Institute provides a wonderful summary that reminds us that each human person as a responsible steward is prohibited from "…self-maiming, destroying a rented apartment, or even having an abortion. This is to say that tenants do not have the same rights as owners. We, as humans, do not own the world, our bodies, or the habitations we rent. Thus, we may improve them but not destroy them."[5]

According to the Torah, not only do women not have the right to do with their bodies as they wish, but neither do men. Our bodies are given to us by a gracious and generous God so that we may occupy them for a certain period of time. During that time they are to be treated with the same deference that a tenant should employ in caring for his rented premises. Similarly, we humans are granted use of the world and all it contains. We may hunt animals for food or clothing, build homes out of the wood we cut from trees and mine the earth to extract the minerals it holds. However, we may not wantonly destroy anything at all.[6] We are to leave our imprint upon the world in a way that improves what we found. This metaphor suggests a gracious land-lord who allows rent-free tenancy in a not yet fully completed home, asking only that its tenants constantly work to improve its condition. Leaving it as we found it is poor repayment for his generosity.[7]

The second most important core value of stewardship involves the growing awareness that our money or treasure is power. Shared treasure and resources create shared power. Churches that share their wealth of money, programs and resources can impact the future of mission churches, grass-root movements of Christian renewal programs and educate the next generation of Christian leaders. Foreign lands that have been plundered and pillaged of their natural resources, civil and tribal wars, rogue soldiers and armies and dictators of political or religious fanaticism can be altered through the generosity of providing financial support to missionaries and service programs providing direct services to the poor. A theology of justly used power and its distribution to those who are powerless are significant benefits to community and culture.

The third most important core value of stewardship is calling each church member by name and using his/her gifts and talents for the work of the community at large. The most underused resource in the Christian church is its laity. Churches that have regular, reliable and varied vehicles for communicating with all church members are forever inviting and encouraging church members to share in the workload of her/his church programs and ministries. Good communication exists in a parish when every household and every member receive regular information about the programs, services and activities of their parish community. The two key words are *every* and *regular*.[8]

Offering church members retreats and workshops that help name their gifts and talents and prayerfully discern their application to church or the church at large is a minimum requirement for an effective stewardship of talents and gifts. This assumes that church leaders and their team have a working knowledge of and familiarity with each church member and can welcome and call them by name. One of the biggest challenges for large churches today is, "How do you remember 1,400+ family names and personally spend the time engaging each member so they feel valued?" Delegation is the answer.

Creating a vibrant team that works with a shared vision of stewardship of talents and gifts enlivens even the most timid and shy church member. An emphasis on time and talent: "this involves completely overhauling many parishes and transforming them into welcoming, hospitable communities that are spiritually dependent on prayer, conduct excellent liturgical celebrations and are obsessed with a desire to give their members good service."[9]

The fourth core value of stewardship is a prayerful community that provides meaningful worship, prayer, spiritual growth and ongoing faith development. As a prayerful community, everything revolves around the parish's eucharistic celebrations (in the Roman Catholic tradition), while other congregations center around the gathering of people to worship and pray. Much time and energy are spent preparing for and celebrating each gathering—particularly those on Saturday and Sunday, when most members assemble to be fed and nurtured through the sacred mysteries, instructed and motivated by the sacred

Scriptures and homilies, and energized by the spirit of the community gathered to worship and praise God. Furthermore, recent stewardship of treasure research indicates that good liturgies and homilies directly and positively impact parish income, as well as parishioners' willingness to share their time and talent.[10]

Eight Levels of Charity

My Grandfather's Blessings, by Rachel Naomi Remen, MD, is a must-read for those who want to understand how God can break through the messiness of life and reveal divine lessons and presence. Dr. Remen recalls her grandfather teaching her the eight levels of charity. She recounts that when a text was subtle and complex, he would simplify all of it but its most basic wisdom. Here is the way that Dr. Remen recalls her grandfather's eight levels of charity.

> At the eighth and most basic level of giving to others, a man begrudgingly buys a coat for a shivering man who has asked him for help, gives it to him in the presence of witnesses, and waits to be thanked.
>
> At the seventh level, a man does this same thing without waiting to be asked for help.
>
> At the sixth level, a man does this same thing openheartedly without waiting to be asked for help.
>
> At the fifth level, a man openheartedly gives a coat that he has bought to another but does so in private.
>
> At the fourth level, a man openheartedly and privately gives his own coat to another, rather than a coat that he has bought.
>
> At the third level, a man openheartedly gives his own coat to another who does not know who has given him this gift. But the man himself knows the person who is indebted to him.
>
> At the second level, he openheartedly gives his own coat to another and has no idea who has received it. But the man who received it knows to whom he is indebted.
>
> And finally, on the first and purest level of giving to others, a man openheartedly gives his own coat away knowing who

will receive it, and he who receives it does not know who has given it to him. Then giving becomes a natural expression of the goodness in us, and we give as simply as flowers breathe out their perfume.[11]

Stewardship for church leaders permeates all of ministry and service. Stewardship at its best invites the people of God to put life, home, work, finances and relationships in order and proportion. The practice of stewardship is giving back to God that which comes from God. Would there be a lack of food, clothing, housing and meaningful employment if each member of every church led a life of order and proportion?

The church leader must be the first in line to embody stewardship as a way of life. This means that each church leader is in charge of his/her daily and weekly schedule and has "authority" over the choices to be made. *Authority* means "…one who authors, owner of the design and the power or right to make final decisions."[12]

- Are you in control of your schedule or does your schedule control you?
- What choices have you made to maintain balance and proportion in your work, family life and ministry?
- You design yourself by the choices you make. Do you like how you designed yourself today?
- Today, look at your schedule; what times did you reserve to meet with God in prayer?
- On your daily schedule of activities have your reserved time and energy to invest in your intimate relationships?
- Have you let those who are your significant love investments know that you value their friendship and relationship?
- Does your use of time allow for moments to ponder, dwell upon, imagine and savor the many blessings that have come your way today?
- Have you taken the time for random acts of kindness with your family, friends, church staff and volunteers, and church members?
- Is it acceptable to linger after a special prayer or worship experience and remember what you appreciated the most about the experience?

- Do you find yourself making the time and effort to say thank you to everyone who comes to your church?
- Are you a good steward of your body, mind, soul and intellect?

Stewardship breeds communal intimacy and vulnerability. The awareness that I cannot do all and be all creates an inclusive attitude that invites the whole community to contribute what they have so as to complete what is needed. Perhaps a willingness to face such shared vulnerability gives us the capacity to repair the world. Those who find the courage to share a common humanity may find they can bless anyone, anywhere.[13]

Dr. Remen tells another story that embodies stewardship at its best. She was on an airplane and realized that a baseball team of seven-year-olds returning from a national baseball competition surrounded her. Seated next to her was a very heavy black woman with a cranky two-year-old. As the plane finally took off, Dr. Remen began a conversation with the woman sitting next to her.

> She began to tell me about the time she spends with the team, the hours of cheering them on, of going door-to-door to raise money for equipment and travel and why she was here now with her two sons. "You can't just keep having kids," she said. "You gotta keep them alive." In her neighborhood many boys were dead or locked away by twenty, victims of drugs or violence. The league was her life insurance for her kids. I looked at her with new respect. She had four, all under the age of ten. The little guy (on her lap) was her baby.
>
> She asked me about my own life, and I told her about my work with people with cancer. Sadness filled her eyes and she began to tell me about her neighbor, a woman like herself, a single mother with four little kids. Six months ago she had been diagnosed with cancer. "The chemo she has to take is terrible," she told me. "It makes her so sick; sometimes she can hardly get out of the bed. I sure hope she can make it through."
>
> She spoke of her neighbor's symptoms, her neighbor's fears, the nightmares that awakened her almost every night.

171

As she unfolded the story, I began to wonder how she knew so many of the intimate details of her neighbor's life, and so I asked her this question. Her answer stunned me. When tragedy had struck next door, she had simply moved her neighbor and all her children into her own home. They had been there for the past five months. I looked at her closely. There was not the slightest air of martyrdom or self-congratulation about her, just this natural reaching out to a person in trouble whose life was next to her own.[14]

A Theology of Stewardship

Church leaders can overlook the intimacy they share ever so frequently and become dull to the marvelous impact they have on those they serve. Practicing the "Prayer of Remembering" can enhance stewardship as a daily event of meeting God in all of life's events. Each day make the time, especially with your staff and core church leaders and ask this simple question, "How have I received or shared a moment of mercy with another in the past 24 hours?" This daily practice of sharing moments of mercy will differentiate the many ways that you have responded in a positive and proactive way to the presence of God.

Excellent Catholic Parishes and *Excellent Protestant Congregations*, both by Paul Wilkes, profile churches that have become living testimonies of the theology of stewardship. The core elements that make an excellent Catholic parish or Protestant congregation are worth reading about, especially the profiles that outline how each church is unique and particular in its application of the key building blocks to its success. I would like to add the following characteristics and qualities that make a church community shine like a beacon and serve as a lighthouse for those who have become lost in the tumultuous waters of life.

1. *Hospitality demonstrated and expected from all levels of church leadership, ministries and membership.*

Reaching out through various communication resources, personal contact, home visits, welcome to newcomers, celebrating anniversaries and other special family and life events, learning the names of church members and calling them by name to volunteer creates that spirit that all are welcome here at the table of plenty. I recently gave a parish mission. At all the weekend masses the rituals of affection shared as parishioners met parishioners and children met their friends demonstrated a church full of hospitality. The smiles, hugs and handshakes were countless. The laughter and exchange of greetings created an atmosphere of care and celebration. I watched how all ages intermingled with one another and when the opening song began it was like walking through a thunderstorm. The power in the voices of all the church members swept me up and lifted me into their spirit of shared praise and rejoicing. Even their choice of the opening song spoke of how well this community can demonstrate hospitality. The opening song was "All Are Welcome."

2. *Sharing resources with those who have less.*

This means that all parish programs and resources have broken through the parochialism and territorialism that have imploded so many churches and congregations. Churches invite members and non-members to share in all aspects of church resources, services and ministries. Churches that are wealthy in money, with multiple programs, trained staff, volunteers and church leadership, share all their resources with their designated sister churches or mission churches. The tithe of time and talent is a call for every church member to share something of what they have with those who don't. Every church member has something to offer of his/her time and talent.

3. *Multiple communities sponsored within the large community.*

It is essential to acknowledge and provide a variety of community and fellowship experiences that allow for specialty groups, focus groups, specific age groups, married, single, widowed or divorced, families with or without children, the home schooled, homebound, cultural and ethnic groups, the sick and disabled, gay and lesbian, and any other life experience that makes a group particular in their need. The church leadership needs to reach out to those who may not fit the usual profile of active and engaged church members. We need to remember that community is always community in the making.

4. *Celebrating a spirituality of joy.*

This permeates every level of church activity. When newcomers walk into a worship service or participate in a workshop or retreat, they are impacted by the joy of the church members and church leaders. Laughter, bantering and teasing with playful and witty nicknames and jokes reflect an intimate knowing of one another.

5. *Worship, music, homilies, and a variety of prayer rituals that meet the spiritual needs of the church members.*

The members bring to prayer the work of their hands. While at parish workdays and specialty work projects church members are at ease about sharing their life struggles, knowing that prayer and intercession are part of the working relationship among church members. The design of worship allows for a variety of expressions and encourages members to go where they are fed. On any given weekend, a variety of worship designs are available to reach out to members with the hope that every person will find at least one type of worship service that will feed and nurture their mind, soul and spirit.

6. *Caring for the poor through direct contact and short-term mission projects.*

This can be achieved through adopting or parish twinning with a church in a second- or third-world country or with a downtown inner-city church. This direct contact allows for church members to share their time, talent and treasure with those who have fewer resources. The giving of time and talent energizes the good steward and realigns his/her awareness that all is gift from God—we are just the stewards.

7. *Faith formation, ongoing education and meeting the growing edge of spirituality.*

Churches that provide for the basic faith and sacramental formation of their children and adults are achieving the minimum to be an effective church. Those churches that invest time, money and personnel to provide ongoing education and stretch the spiritual comfort zone of their church membership will call forth the next generation of mystics, saints and prophets. Remember that there is no growth in holiness without self-knowledge (Teresa of Avila). There is no growth in the same, the familiar and the known. At best you may achieve some mastery and refinement. Growth begins with the uncomfortable, the unknown and the unfamiliar. When a person is led to their growing edge, the treasure hunting for potential begins. Providing teachers, mentors and spiritual directors to help others deepen their faith and spiritual life assumes that the church leader is comfortable with exploring his/her growing edge, allowing others to take the lead while they follow.

8. *Sharing responsibilities for all matters of church life and embracing ownership of the success and failures of church life.*

Corporations around the world have discovered that when employees take pride and ownership in their workplace there is a direct relationship in their willingness to sacrifice and go the extra mile; an increase in quality of work performance prevails; commitment to the well-being of others is demonstrated; a desire to contribute to problem solving and being proactive toward company and employee issues become the welcomed attitude among owner, manager and employee. When church members feel that their ideas and suggestions are heard, and receive a response, they will want to do more, give more and care more for their church. Every church member needs to be welcomed as a contributor to the health and well-being of all the dimensions of the church; otherwise, apathy grows and a lack of interest atrophies any possible empathy. The absence of empathy breeds chronic criticisms, sabotage, indifference, casual commitments and a drive-through restaurant mentality.

9. *Environmental stewardship.*

Do your church members contribute to the healing of the earth? Is your congregation directly involved with protecting God's gift of creation and educating the next generation about being good tenants of an earth that has been given to us on loan? Basic to environmental stewardship is replenishing what we take from the earth. Does your parish recycle? Have you made a congregational commitment to collectively advocate for eco-friendly resources, purchase fair-trade products, learn about water conservation, advocate for plants and trees that enhance the production of clean air, and purchase green products so as to reduce waste and disposal? Can you imagine what would happen if churches banded together for one small environmental cause? Together we could make an impact on our neighborhoods, counties, states and country that would send ripples worldwide that we are effective stewards of the natural resources God has provided and that we invite the world community to join in our efforts.

In a small town outside of a large California city, I met a young twelve-year-old boy who got the idea to ask his neighbors if they would allow him to take their oranges that had fallen to the ground and sell them to raise money for an orphanage he had heard about in Africa. The neighbors applauded this young boy's energy and generosity to serve abandoned children in Africa and began to donate other fruits that fell to the ground. In time, this young boy had collected a large selection of fruits and had an extensive distribution network of family, friends and others who benefited from the purchase of fruit that may have had a few bruises, yet was still fresh and usable, while supporting this young boy's campaign to raise money for an orphanage. This is a simple example of environmental stewardship.

Many people who shop for fruits and vegetables in our major cities have little or no idea what real fresh fruit and vegetables look like. Real fresh fruits and vegetables come with imperfections, maybe some bruises, but without the plastic coating or protective sprays, pesticides, stamped numbers or commercial wrapping. How do we educate our church members to walk close to the earth, eat food that is natural and avoid processed foods without risk of bacteria or other contaminants? How do we educate our church members so that they are not duped by the commercialism that says, "More is better, so make that extra large or double the size." Most Americans could reduce their food intake by 50 percent and still not go hungry. How do we eat less so that others may have a simple meal? How do Christians share fairly in the distribution of goods so that others may struggle less with survival? Recently in a magazine article dealing with how much Americans use of our world resources, it was mentioned that the food garbage that we throw away as a nation in one day could feed thirty-five million hungry people three complete meals for one day.

As the United States Catholic Conference explains, humans bear "a unique responsibility under God: to safeguard the created world by their creative labor, even to enhance it." Hence, the good steward does not allow the resources entrusted to him to lie fallow or fail to produce fruit. Nor does he destroy them irrevocably. Rather, he uses them, develops them and, to the best of his ability, strives to realize an increase so that he may enjoy his livelihood and provide for the good of his family and his descendants.[15]

Stewardship lived as a chosen way of life is empowering. Stewardship lived as a chosen way of life as a church can be revolutionary in its impact on families, friends, neighborhoods and our country. Stewardship lived as a chosen way of life is the embodiment of the Word of God. We become eucharistic bread for a hungry world. Miracles abound in the lives and homes of those who choose stewardship as a way of life.

Additional Resources

Consult the bibliography for complete publishing information on the following titles:

Acton Institute. *Environmental Stewardship in the Judeo-Christian Tradition.*

Clements, C. Justin. *The Steward's Way: A Spirituality of Stewardship.*

Hoge, Dean, R. *The First Five Years of the Priesthood: A Study of Newly Ordained Catholic Priests.*

Remen, Rachel Naomi, MD. *My Grandfather's Blessings: Stories of Strength, Refuge, and Belonging.*

Tannen, Deborah. *Talking from 9 to 5.*

Wilkes, Paul. *Excellent Catholic Parishes: The Guide to the Best Places and Practices.*

————. *Excellent Protestant Congregations.*

Chapter 19
Creating a Health-Care Plan
Investing in the Pastoral Leader

Health-Care Plan for Living Life to the Full

To manage a daily regime of balance and proportion, list five examples of how you will live out each of the following statements. *For the complete plan, see online handout 13, Health-Care Plan for Living Life to the Full.* [To access: www.paulistpress.com, Online Resources, book title] Imagine creating a menu that allows you to choose from a selection of healthy ways to maintain balance and proportion. You are the architect of your health-care plan. Be creative and innovative in your choice making, so that you are nourished and encouraged to live "life…to the full" (John 10:10).

Core Values to Living Healthy:
The Vibrant Person, Family, Congregation, Workplace and Society

Take some quiet time and ask yourself, "Do I need more or less of each dimension of the core values to living healthy as a vibrant person?" You can use the same exercise for your family, congregation and workplace.

Wholeness–How do you care for your body, mind, spirit and soul?

"May the God of peace make you perfect in holiness."
1 Thessalonians 5:23

More of		Less of
	Physical	
	Emotional	
	Spiritual	
	Social	
	Intellectual	

Growth–Are you being stretched and challenged?

Living "life…to the full."
John 10:10

More of		Less of
	Physical	
	Emotional	
	Spiritual	
	Social	
	Intellectual	

Protection–How do you defend and protect yourself and others?

"Put on the armor of God…."
Ephesians 6:11

More of		Less of
	Physical	
	Emotional	
	Spiritual	
	Social	
	Intellectual	

Nourishment—How do you nurture yourself?

"An invitation to grace."
Isaiah 55:1–4

More of	**Less of**
Physical	
Emotional	
Spiritual	
Social	
Intellectual	

My Personal Health-Care Plan

These are the new patterns of thinking, feeling, desiring and behaving that I would like to achieve. I will ask five people to call me weekly and hold me accountable to my health-care plan so that I can achieve these new goals.

- Physical
- Spiritual
- Emotional
- Social
- Intellectual
- Family
- Employment
- Ministry

Notes

Introduction

1. *A Pictorial History of the Boyne Valley Area* (Boyne Falls, MI: The Centennial Book Committee, n.d.), 53.

Chapter 1: Men and Women in Ministry: Honoring the Differences

1. Deborah Tannen, *Talking from 9 to 5* (New York: William Morrow, 1994), 307.

2. Ibid., 308–9.

3. Deborah Tannen, *You Just Don't Understand: Women and Men in Conversation* (New York: Harper, 1990), 16.

4. This chart is included in Deborah Tannen's video, *Talking from 9 to 5: Women and Men in the Workplace*, video booklet, 24 (distributed by ChartHouse International Learning in Burnsville, MN; 800-328-3789).

5. Tannen, *You Just Don't Understand*, 42.

6. Ibid., 38.

Chapter 2: Rituals of Affection, and Internal and External Boundaries

1. Henry Cloud and John Townsend, *Boundaries* (Grand Rapids: Zondervan, 1992), 65.

2. William J. Jarema, *Fathering the Next Generation: Men Mentoring Men* (New York: Crossroad, 2003), summary review.

Chapter 3: How to Create a Hostile Work Environment in Ten Easy Steps

1. Michele A. Paludi and Richard B. Barickman, *Academic and Workplace Sexual Harassment: A Resource Manual* (Albany: State University of New York Press, 1991), 7.
2. Ibid., 6.
3. Ibid., 4.
4. Ibid., 3.
5. Ibid., 12.
6. Ibid., 13.

Chapter 4: Dual Relationships and the Continuum of Social Relationships

1. Barbara Herlihy and Gerald Corey, *Dual Relationships in Counseling* (Alexandria, VA: American Association for Counseling and Development, 1992), 7.
2. Ibid., xiii.
3. Ibid.
4. Ibid., 23.

Chapter 5: Confidential, Privileged Information, Private-Internal Forum and Public-External Forum

1. *Webster's Unabridged Dictionary*, 2nd ed. (New York: Random House, 1983), 382.
2. Ibid., 1640.
3. John P. Beal, James A Coriden, and Thomas J. Green, eds., *New Commentary on the Canon Law* (New York / Mahwah, NJ: Paulist Press, 2000), canon 240, par. 2.
4. Peter M. J. Stravinskas, *The Catholic Answer Book 3* (Huntington, IN: Our Sunday Visitor, 1998), 152.
5. United States Conference of Catholic Bishops, *Program of Priestly Formation*, 5th ed. (Washington, DC: USCCB), par. 134.

Chapter 6: The Power Shadow in the Helping Professions

1. Adolf Guggenbuhl-Craig, *Power in the Helping Professions* (Dallas: Spring Publications, 1990), vii.

2. Ibid., 7.

3. Ibid., 9.

4. Ibid., 15.

5. Ibid., 31–32.

6. Ibid., 76–77.

7. "Fatima: The Secret's Out, Despite Claims to the Contrary," by Cindy Wooden, CNS, May 11, 2007.

8. Peter McWilliams, *Life 101: Everything We Wish We Had Learned About Life in School—But Didn't* (Algonac, Michigan: Mary Books/Prelude Press, 1994), 214.

9. Ibid., 57.

10. Ibid., 135.

11. Ibid., 151.

12. Ibid., 154.

13. Robert A. Johnson, *Owning Your Own Shadow* (San Francisco: HarperCollins, 1996), 19.

Chapter 7: Pastoral Leaders and Projections: Fatal-Attraction Syndrome, Understanding Infatuations and Repulsions

1. *A Safe Home* (Parent's Place, 1992), source unknown.

2. Robert A. Johnson, *Owning Your Own Shadow* (San Francisco: HarperCollins, 1996), 31.

3. Mark Miller, sales manager, October 2007, *Bits & Pieces*: Ragan's Motivational Resources, 111 E. Wacker Dr., Ste. 500, Chicago, IL. 60601; phone: 800-878-5331; e-mail: motivate@ragan.com.

Chapter 8: He Said—She Said—They Said: Patterns of Dysfunctional Communication

1. *Christian Communication Covenant*, written by Rev. William J. Jarema.
2. "Christian Response to Conflict," source unknown.
3. "Seven A's of Confession," source unknown.
4. "Four Promises of Forgiveness," source unknown.
5. William Ellery Channing (1780–1842), cleric, November 2007, *Bits & Pieces*: Ragan's Motivational Resources, 111 E. Wacker Dr., Ste. 500, Chicago, IL. 60601; phone: 800-878-5331; e-mail: motivate@ragan.com.
6. Webster's Unabridged Dictionary, Deluxe Second Edition, 1983.
7. Ibid.

Chapter 12: Why Do People Gossip?

1. *Leadership with a Human Touch*, vol. G, no. 4 (Fairfield, NJ: Economics Press, n.d.), 66.
2. *Clergy Talk*, July 2007. P.O. Box 1809, Sequim, WA 98382-1809. Fax 360-683-7448; e-mail clergytalk@wavecable.com; phone 360-683-2426.

Chapter 13: Counseling and Spiritual Direction: Do's and Don'ts

1. Spiritual Directors International Web site: www.sdiworld.org; P.O. Box 3584, Bellevue, WA 98009-3584; or membership@sdiworld.org.
2. American Psychotherapy Association Web site: www.americanpsychotherapy.com.
3. American Association for Marriage and Family Therapy at www.aamft.org or AAMFT, 112 South Alfred Street, Alexandria, VA 22314-3061. Phone: 703-838-9808; fax: 703-838-9805. Also see FamilyTherapyResources.net, a public service of the AAMFT.
4. The Association for Clinical Pastoral Education, Inc., Web site: www.acpe.edu.
5. Professional Chaplaincy Web site: www.healthcarechaplaincy.org.

Chapter 17: Ministry Burnout: Red Flags and Warning Signs

1. Dean R Hoge, *The First Five Years of the Priesthood: A Study of Newly Ordained Catholic Priests* (Collegeville, MN: Liturgical Press, 2002), 63.

2. Ibid., 63–64.

3. Spirit Mercy Prayer, Rev. William J. Jarema, 1987. The prayer for the Society of Missionaries of Mercy. Used with permission.

Chapter 18: Stewardship: Responding to God's Generosity

1. Justin Clements, *The Steward's Way: A Spirituality of Stewardship*, (Kansas City: Sheed & Ward, 1997), 91.

2. Ibid., 85.

3. Ibid., 29.

4. Ibid., viii.

5. Acton Institute, *Environmental Stewardship in the Judeo-Christian Tradition* (Acton Institute, Ottawa Avenue NW, Suite 301, Grand Rapids, MI 49503-2008; www.acton.org), 21.

6. Ibid., 21.

7. Ibid., 24.

8. Justin Clements, *The Steward's Way: A Spirituality of Stewardship* (Kansas City: Sheed & Ward, 1997), 44.

9. Ibid., 25.

10. Ibid., 36.

11. Rachel Naomi Remen, *My Grandfather's Blessings* (New York: Riverhead Books, 2001), 86–87.

12. *Webster's Unabridged Dictionary*, 1983.

13. Remen, *My Grandfather's Blessings* 105.

14. Ibid., 94.

15. Acton Institute, *Environmental Stewardship in the Judeo-Christian Tradition* (Acton Institute, Ottawa Avenue, NW, Suite 301, Grand Rapids, MI 49503-2008; www.acton.org), 39–40.

Bibliography

Acton Institute. *Environmental Stewardship in the Judeo-Christian Tradition*. Acton Institute, Ottawa Ave. NW, Suite 301, Grand Rapids, MI 49503-2008; www.acton.org.

ADL Associates. *Back to Basics*. Dallas: CornerStone Leadership Institute, 2003.

Allen, Marc. *The Ten Percent Solution*. Novato, CA: New World Library, 2002.

Aron, Elaine N. *The Highly Sensitive Person*. New York: Broadway Books, 1996.

Baldoni, John. *180 Ways to Walk the Leadership Talk*. Dallas: The Walk the Talk Company, 2000.

Bassett, Lucinda. *From Panic to Power*. New York: Collins Wellness, HarperCollins, 1995.

Bausch, William J. *The Parish of the Next Millennium*. Mystic, CT: Twenty-Third Publications, 1997.

Begolly, Michael J. *Leading the Assembly in Prayer*. San Jose, CA: Resource Publications, 1997.

Bilanich, Bud. *Leading with Values*. Dallas: The Walk the Talk Company, 2004.

Blair, Gary Ryan. *Goal Setting for Results*. Dallas: The Walk the Talk Company, 2003.

Boyle, Victor J. *60 Winning Skills for Parish Leaders*. Malvern, NY: Applied Leadership Research, 2000.

Bradshaw, John. *The Family: A New Way of Creating Solid Self-Esteem*. Deerfield Beach, FL: Health Communications, 1988.

Briner, Bob, and Ray Pritchard. *Leadership Lessons of Jesus*. New York: Gramercy Books, 1998.

Brown, Richard C. *When Ministry Is Messy*. Cincinnati: St. Anthony Messenger Press, 2006.

Buckingham, Marcus, and Donald O. Clifton. *Now, Discover Your Strengths*. New York: The Free Press, Simon & Schuster, 2001.

Bushe, Gervase R. *Clear Leadership*. Palo Alto, CA: Davies-Black Publishing, 2001.

Callahan, Kennon L. *Effective Church Leadership*. San Francisco: Harper & Row, 1990.

————. *Twelve Keys to an Effective Church*. San Francisco: Jossey-Bass, 1983.

Carnegie, Dale, and Associates. *Managing Through People*. New York: Simon & Schuster, 1975.

Ciarrocchi, Joseph W. *A Minister's Handbook of Mental Disorders*. Mahwah, NJ: Paulist Press, 1993.

Clark, Stephen B. *Building Christian Communities*. Notre Dame, Indiana: Ave Maria Press, 1972.

Clements, C. Justin. *The Steward's Way: A Spirituality of Stewardship*. Kansas City: Sheed & Ward, 1997.

Cloud, Henry, and John Townsend. *Boundaries*. Grand Rapids, MI: Zondervan, 1992.

————. *Setting Boundaries With Your Adult Children*. Eugene, OR: Harvest House Publishers, 2008.

Cohen, William A. *The Stuff of Heroes*. Atlanta: Longstreet Publishers, 1998.

Colan, Lee J. *Sticking to It*. Dallas: CornerStone Leadership Institute, 2003.

Considine, John J. *Marketing Your Church*. Kansas City: Sheed & Ward, 1995.

Cook, J. Keith, and Lee C. Moorehead. *Six Stages of a Pastor's Life*. Nashville: Abingdon Press, 1990.

Cottrell, David. *12 Choices That Lead to Your Success*. Dallas: CornerStone Leadership Institute, 2005.

Covey, Stephen R. *Principle-Centered Leadership*. New York: Fireside, Simon & Schuster, 1990.

Crosby, Michael H. *The Dysfunctional Church*. Notre Dame, IN: Ave Maria Press, 1991.

————. *Spirituality of the Beatitudes*. Maryknoll, NY: Orbis Books, 1981.

Cruse, Sharon Wegscheider. *Choice Making for Codependents, Adult Children and Spirituality Seekers*. Pampana Beach, FL: Health Communications, 1985.

Dargatz, Jan. *Women and Power*. Atlanta: Thomas Nelson Publishers, 1995.

DeCarlo, Donald T., and Deborah H. Gruenfeld. *Stress in the American Workplace: Alternatives for the Working Wounded*. Fort Washington, PA: LRP Publications, 1989.

Deci, Edward L., and Richard Flaste. *Why We Do What We Do: Understanding Self-Motivation*. New York: Penguin Books, 1995.

Deegan, Arthur X. *Developing a Vibrant Parish Pastoral Council*. Mahwah, NJ: Paulist Press, 1995.

DeSiano, Frank, and Kenneth Boyack. *Creating the Evangelizing Parish*. Mahwah, NJ: Paulist Press, 1993.

Dodds, Bill, and Michael, OP. *Living the Beatitudes Today: Happily Ever After Begins Here and Now*. Chicago: Loyola Press, 1997.

Dubitsky, Cora Marie. *Building the Faith Community*. Mahwah, NJ: Paulist Press, 1974.

Engstrom, Ted W. *The Making of a Christian Leader*. Grand Rapids: Zondervan, 1976.

Faller, Tod. *It's All About YOU!* Bloomington, IN: 1st Books Library, 2002.

Ferder, Fran, and John Heagle. *Partnership: Women and Men in Ministry*. Notre Dame, IN: Ave Maria Press, 1989.

Finzel, Hans. *The Top Ten Mistakes Leaders Make*. Colorado Springs, Co: Cook Communications Ministries, 1994.

Forest, Jim. *The Ladder of the Beatitudes*. Maryknoll, NY: Orbis Books, 1999.

Forster, Patricia M., and Thomas P. Sweetser. *Transforming the Parish*. Kansas City: Sheed & Ward, 1993.

Gardner, John W. *On Leadership*. New York: The Free Press, Macmillan, 1990.

Geaney, Dennis. *Full Church, Empty Rectory*. Notre Dame, IN: Fides/Claretian, 1980.

Guggenbuhl-Craig, Adolf. *Power in the Helping Professions*. Dallas: Spring Publications, 1971.

Guzie, Tad, and Noreen Monroe. *About Men & Women: How Your "Great Story" Shapes Your Destiny*. Mahwah, NJ: Paulist Press, 1986.

Hackman, Michael Z., and Craig E. Johnson. *Leadership: A Communication Perspective*. Prospect Heights, IL: Waveland Press, 1991.

Haring, Bernard, CSSR. *The Blessed Beatitudes: Salt and Light*. Liguori, MO: Liguori Publications, 1999.

Harvey, Eric, and Al Lucia. *144 Ways to Walk the Talk*. Dallas: The Walk the Talk Company, 1999.

Harvey, Eric, and the Walk the Talk Team. *180 Ways to Walk the Customer Service Talk*. Dallas: The Walk the Talk Company, 1999.

Harvey, Eric, and Steve Ventura. *Walk Awhile in My Shoes*. Dallas: The Walk the Talk Company, 2003.

Harvey, Joan C., and Cynthia Katz. *If I'm So Successful Why Do I Feel Like a Fake?* New York: St. Martin's Press, 1985.

Haughey, John C. *Personal Values in Public Policy*. Mahwah, NJ: Paulist Press, 1979.

Herlihy, Barbara, and Gerald Corey. *Dual Relationships in Counseling*. Alexandria, VA: American Association for Counseling and Development, 1992.

Hickman, Craig R. *Mind of a Manager, Soul of a Leader*. New York: John Wiley & Sons, 1990.

Hinnebusch, Paul. *The Beatitudes: Seeking the Joy of God's Kingdom*. Boston: Pauline Books & Media, 2000.

Hoge, Dean. *Future of Catholic Leadership*. Kansas City: Sheed & Ward, 1987.

Hoge, Dean, Jackson W. Carroll, and Francis K. Scheets. *Patterns of Parish Leadership*. Kansas City: Sheed & Ward, 1988.

Jarema, William. *Conscious Celibacy: Truth or Consequences*. Colorado Springs, CO: The Mercy Center, 2007.

————. *Fathering the Next Generation*. New York: Crossroad, 1994.

————. *There's a Hole in My Chest*. New York: Crossroad, 1996.

Johnson, Robert A. *Owning Your Own Shadow*. New York: Harper-SanFrancisco, 1991.

————. *We*. New York: HarperCollins, 1983.

Jones, Dewitt. *Celebrate What's Right With the World* (DVD). Star Thrower, 26 East Exchange Street, Suite 600, St. Paul, MN 55101 or 800-242-3220 or www.starthrower.com.

Katzenbach, Jon R. *Why Pride Matters More Than Money*. New York: Crown Business, 2003.

Keating, Charles J. *Dealing with Difficult People*. Mahwah, NJ: Paulist Press, 1984.

Keirsey, David, and Marilyn Bates. *Please Understand Me*. Del Mar, CA: Prometheus Nemesis Books, 1978.

Knell, Marion. *Burn Up or Splash Down: Surviving the Culture Shock of Re-Entry*. Atlanta: Authentic, 2006.

Kouzes, James, and Barry Posner. *The Leadership Challenge*. San Francisco: Jossey-Bass, 2002.

Lamdin, Keith, and David Tilley. *Supporting New Ministers in the Local Church*. London: SPCK, 2007.

The Leadership Success Set. Shawnee Mission, KS: National Press Publications, 1990.
—*Getting Things Done*
—*How to Manage Conflict*
—*Positive Performance Management*
—*The Supervisor's Handbook*
—*Team Building*
—*Techniques of Successful Delegation*

Lehr, Fred. *Clergy Burnout: Recovering From the 70-hour Work Week...and Other Self-Defeating Practices*. Minneapolis: Fortress Press, 2006.

Linn, Matthew, Sheila Fabricant Linn, and Dennis Linn. *Healing Spiritual Abuse and Religious Addiction*. Mahwah, NJ: Paulist Press, 1994.

London, H. B., Jr., and Neil B. Wiseman. *Pastors at Greater Risk: Real Help From Pastors Who've Been There*. Ventura, CA: Regal Books, From Gospel Light, 2003.

Lucado, Max. *3:16—The Numbers of Hope*. Nashville: Thomas Nelson, 2007.

Ludeman, Kate, and Eddie Erlandson. *Alpha Male Syndrome*. Boston: Harvard Business School Press, 2006.

Lutz, Robert R., and Bruce T. Taylor. *Surviving in Ministry*. Mahwah, NJ: Paulist Press, 1990.

Maxwell, John C. *The 360-Degree Leader*. Nashville, Tennessee: Nelson Business, A Division of Thomas Nelson Publishers, 2005.

———. *Be a People Person*. Colorado Springs, CO: Cook Communications Ministries, 2004.

———. *Developing the Leader Within You*. Nashville, Tennessee: Thomas Nelson, Inc., 1993.

————. *The 21 Irrefutable Laws of Leadership*. Nashville, Tennessee: Thomas Nelson Publishers, 1998.

McGraw, Phillip. *Life Strategies*. New York: Hyperion, 1999.

McKenna, Kevin E. *A Concise Guide to Your Rights in the Catholic Church*. Notre Dame, IN: Ave Maria Press, 2006.

McKenna, Megan. *Blessings and Woe*. Maryknoll, New York: Orbis Books, 1999.

Minirth, Frank, Paul Meier, and Don Hawkins,. *Worry Free Living*. Carmel, New York: Guideposts, 1989.

Nielsen, Duke. *Partnering with Employees*. San Francisco: Jossey-Bass, 1993.

Nierenberg, Gerard I. *The Art of Negotiating*. New York: Simon & Schuster, 1968.

Paludi, Michele A., and Richard B. Barickman. *Academic and Workplace Sexual Harassment*. Albany: State University of New York Press, 1991.

Perry, Charles, Jr. *Why Christians Burn Out*. Nashville: Thomas Nelson Publishers, 1982.

Riley, Mary. *Corporate Healing*. Deerfield Beach, FL: Heath Communications, 1990.

Robinson, Bryan E. *Work Addiction*. Deerfield Beach, FL: Heath Communications, 1989.

Rutz, James H. *The Open Church*. Beaumount, TX: The Seedsowers, 1992.

Sanford, John A. *The Invisible Partners: How the Male and Female in Each of Us Affects Our Relationship*. Mahwah, NJ: Paulist Press, 1980.

————. *Ministry Burnout*. Louisville: KY: Westminster/John Knox Press, 1982.

Schaef, Anne Wilson. *When Society Becomes an Addict*. San Francisco: Harper & Row, 1987.

Schaeffer, Brenda. *Is It Love or Is It Addiction?* Center City, MN: Hazelden Educational Materials, 1987.

Smith, Hyrum. *The 10 Natural Laws of Successful Time and Life Management*. New York: Warner Books, 1994.

Swain, Bernard. *Liberating Leadership*. San Francisco: Harper & Row, 1986.

Sweetser, Thomas, SJ, and Carol Wisniewski Holden. *Leadership in a Successful Parish*. San Francisco: Harper & Row, 1987.

Tannen, Deborah. *Talking from 9 to 5*. New York: William Morrow, 1994.

————. *That's Not What I Meant: How Conversational Style Makes or Breaks Relationships*. New York: Ballantine Books, 1991.

————. *You Just Don't Understand : Women and Men in Conversation*. New York: Harper, 1990.

Templar, Richard. *The Rules of Management*. Harlow, England: Pearson, Prentice-Hall Business, 2005.

————. *The Rules of Work*. Upper Saddle River, NJ: Pearson, Prentice-Hall, 2005.

Thomas, Marlin. *Resolving Disputes in Christian Groups*. Winnipeg, Manitoba, Canada: Wildflower Communications, 1994.

Thomas, Oliver. *10 Things Your Minister Wants to Tell You But Can't Because He Needs the Job*. New York: St. Martin's Press, 2007.

Tieger, Paul D., and Barbara B. *Do What You Are*. New York: Little, Brown and Company, 1992.

Vanier, Jean. *Community and Growth*. Mahwah, NJ: Paulist Press, 1979.

Ventura, Steve. *Start Right, Stay Right*. Dallas: The Walk the Talk Company, 2004.

Walk the Talk Resources. *The Leadership Secrets of Santa Claus*. Dallas: The Walk the Talk Company, 2003.

————. *Leading with Values*. Dallas: The Walk the Talk Company, 2003.

White, Joseph D., PhD. *Burnout Busters: Stress Management for Ministry*. Huntington, IN: Our Sunday Visitor, 2007.

Wilkes, Paul. *Excellent Catholic Parishes*. Mahwah, NJ: Paulist Press, 2001.

————. *Excellent Protestant Congregations*. New York/Mahwah, NJ: Paulist Press, 2001.

Wilson, Michael Todd, and Brad Hoffman. *Preventing Ministry Failure*. Downers Grove, IL: IVP Books, 2007.

Wilson, Richard. *The Journey of the Beatitudes*. Center City, MN: Hazelden Educational Materials, 1986.

Wilson-Schaef, Anne. *When Society Becomes An Addict*. San Francisco: Harper & Row, 1987.

Wilson-Schaef, Anne, and Diane Fassel. *The Addictive Organization*. San Francisco: Harper & Row, 1988.

Winseman, Albert L., Donald O. Clifton, and Curt Liesveld. *Living Your Strengths*. New York: Gallup Press, 2003.

Woititz, Janet Geringer. *Struggle for Intimacy*. Pompano Beach, FL: Health Communications, 1985.

Yager, Jan, PhD. *When Friendship Hurts: How to Deal With Friends Who Betray, Abandon, or Wound You*. New York: Simon & Schuster, Fireside Books, 2002.